University of Cambridge Oriental Publications No. 41

Molech: A god of human sacrifice in the Old Testament

Molech

A god of human sacrifice in the Old Testament

JOHN DAY

Fellow and Tutor of Lady Margaret Hall
and Lecturer in Old Testament in the University of Oxford

The right of the University of Cambridge to print and sell all manner of books was granted by Henry VIII in 1534. The University has printed and published continuously since 1584.

CAMBRIDGE UNIVERSITY PRESS

CAMBRIDGE

NEW YORK NEW ROCHELLE MELBOURNE SYDNEY

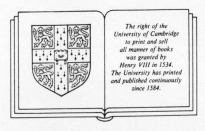

Published by the Press Syndicate of the University of Cambridge
The Pitt Building, Trumpington Street, Cambridge CB2 1RP
32 East 57th Street, New York, NY 10022, USA
10 Stamford Road, Oakleigh, Melbourne 3166, Australia

First published 1989

Printed in Great Britain at The Bath Press, Avon

British Library cataloguing in publication data

Day, John, *1948–*
Molech: a god of human sacrifice in the Old
Testament.
1. Judaism. Idols. Moloch
I. Title II. Series
296

Library of Congress cataloguing in publication data

Day, John, 1948–
Molech: a god of human sacrifice in the Old Testament / by John Day.
p. cm. – (University of Cambridge oriental publications: no. 41)
Bibliography.
Includes index.
ISBN 0-521-36474-4
1. Molech (Semitic deity) 2. Sacrifice, Human–Biblical teaching.
3. Bible. O.T. – Criticism, interpretation, etc. I. Title.
II. Series.
BL 1605.M6D39 1989
299′.26—dc19 89-30403 CIP

ISBN 0 521 36474 4

VN

CONTENTS

PREFACE

The present study arises out of several years of research on the Molech cult. I had originally intended it to be but one chapter in a book on the gods of Canaan and the Old Testament, but as my interest in Molech developed and my material grew, I decided to devote a whole monograph to the subject.

The manuscript of this book was essentially finished before the publication of G. C. Heider's *The Cult of Molek: A Reassessment* (Sheffield, dated 1985, but actually appeared 1986). It is interesting to observe that we independently came to the same conclusions on a number of the central questions. However, many of the arguments employed and a large number of the topics raised in my study do not feature in his book, and there are also points on which we differ.

I am grateful to Professor J. A. Emerton of Cambridge, Professor D. Pardee of Chicago, and the Revd. B. A. Mastin of Bangor, who kindly read through an earlier draft of this study and made valuable suggestions for its improvement. I am also indebted to Dr Gordon Johnson and the Faculty of Oriental Studies Publications Committee for accepting this work for inclusion in their series.

ABBREVIATIONS

AJSL	*American Journal of Semitic Languages and Literatures*
ANET	J. B. Pritchard (ed.), *Ancient Near Eastern Texts Relating to the Old Testament*, 3rd edn (Princeton, 1969)
AOAT	*Alter Orient und Altes Testament*
ASOR	*American Schools of Oriental Research*
AV	*Authorized Version*
BARev	*Biblical Archaeology Review*
BASOR	*Bulletin of the American Schools of Oriental Research*
BDB	F. Brown, S. R. Driver, and C. A. Briggs, *A Hebrew and English Lexicon of the Old Testament* (Oxford, 1907; reprinted with corrections, 1953)
BSOAS	*Bulletin of the School of Oriental and African Studies*
BWANT	*Beiträge zur Wissenschaft vom Alten und Neuen Testament*
BZAW	*Beihefte zur Zeitschrift für die alttestamentliche Wissenschaft*
CBQ	*Catholic Biblical Quarterly*
CILat	*Corpus Inscriptionum Latinarum*
CIS	*Corpus Inscriptionum Semiticarum*
CRAIBL	*Comptes rendus des séances de l'Académie des Inscriptions & Belles-Lettres*
CT	*Cuneiform Texts from Babylonian Tablets, &c., in the British Museum*
CTA	A. Herdner, *Corpus des tablettes en cunéiformes alphabétiques* (2 vols., Paris, 1963)
ET	English translation
HTR	*Harvard Theological Review*
HUCA	*Hebrew Union College Annual*
JA	*Journal Asiatique*
JANESCU	*Journal of the Ancient Near Eastern Society of Columbia University*
JAOS	*Journal of the American Oriental Society*
JBL	*Journal of Biblical Literature*
JNES	*Journal of Near Eastern Studies*

JPOS	*Journal of the Palestine Oriental Society*
JTS	*Journal of Theological Studies*
KAI	H. Donner and W. Röllig, *Kanaanäische und aramäische Inschriften* (3 vols., Wiesbaden, 1966–9)
KB	L. Koehler and W. Baumgartner, *Lexicon in Veteris Testamenti Libros* (Leiden, 1958)
KTU	M. Dietrich, O. Loretz, and J. Sanmartín, *Die keilalphabetischen Texte aus Ugarit. Teil 1: Transkription* (*AOAT* 24, Neukirchen-Vluyn, 1976)
LXX	Septuagint
MT	Massoretic text
NAB	*New American Bible*
NEB	*New English Bible*
NS	New Series
OTS	*Oudtestamentische Studiën*
PEQ	*Palestine Exploration Quarterly*
RA	*Revue d'Assyriologie*
RB	*Revue Biblique*
RES	*Répertoire d'épigraphie Sémitique*
RHR	*Revue de l'Histoire des Religions*
RIH	*Ras Ibn Hani*
RS	*Ras Shamra*
RSF	*Rivista di Studi Fenici*
RSO	*Rivista degli Studi Orientali*
RSV	*Revised Standard Version*
RV	*Revised Version*
SBL	*Society of Biblical Literature*
SVT	*Supplements to Vetus Testamentum*
TGUOS	*Transactions of the Glasgow University Oriental Society*
ThLZ	*Theologische Literaturzeitung*
UF	*Ugarit-Forschungen*
VT	*Vetus Testamentum*
WMANT	*Wissenschaftliche Monographien zum Alten und Neuen Testament*
ZAW	*Zeitschrift für die alttestamentliche Wissenschaft*
ZDMG	*Zeitschrift der deutschen morgenländischen Gesellschaft*
ZDPV	*Zeitschrift des deutschen Palästina-Vereins*

INTRODUCTION

The subject of the present monograph is the Molech cult in the Old Testament. It is a topic on which a considerable amount has been written over the years, although the number of complete monographs devoted to it is very small.[1]

Explicit references to the Molech cult are relatively rare in the Old Testament. They may be found in Lev. 18.21, 20.2–5; Jer. 32.35 and 2 Kgs. 23.10.[2] However, as we shall see, there are also a number of other implicit references (e.g. Isa. 30.33, 57.9; Jer. 7.31, 19.5; and perhaps Zeph. 1.5), including one which has never hitherto been noticed (Isa. 28.15, 18). Nevertheless, although the number of references is relatively small, it is clearly a subject on which the Old Testament writers felt very strongly, and the Molech cult was regarded as a particularly heinous practice to which Yahweh was implacably opposed.

Although a fair amount has already been written on this subject, there is still controversy about the main questions which it raises. It is this fact which provides the justification for the present monograph, in which an attempt will be made to chart a way through the sea of conflicting views.

The first question which arises is whether Molech is the name of a god at all. This was generally assumed as self-evident until 1935,[3]

1 In the present century there have been O. Eissfeldt, *Molk als Opferbegriff im Punischen und Hebräischen und das Ende des Gottes Moloch* (Halle, 1935); K. Dronkert, *De Molochdienst in het Oude Testament* (Leiden, 1953); G. C. Heider, *The Cult of Molek: A Reassessment* (Sheffield, 1985).

2 The MT of 1 Kgs. 11.7 also refers to Molech but it is generally accepted that we should emend to Milcom. Cf. pp. 32 and 74.

3 The main earlier discussions relevant to the question of Molech are as follows: J. Selden, *Die diis Syris* (London, 1617), syntagma 1, ch. 6; T. Godwin, *Moses and Aaron* (London, 1625), bk. 4, ch. 2; J. Spencer, *De Legibus Hebraeorum Ritualibus* (Cambridge, 1685), bk. 3, ch. 13; H. Wits (Witsius), *Miscellaneorum sacrorum libri iv.* 2nd edn (Amsterdam, 1695), bk. 2, diss. 5; J. Braun, *Selecta sacra*

when Eissfeldt argued in an influential work that Molech is rather a sacrificial term, cognate with Punic *molk*. Not all scholars have followed Eissfeldt's interpretation, however, and, as we shall see, it is indeed open to serious doubt.

A further question on which there is dispute concerns the nature of the cult. The Old Testament condemns the practice of what has traditionally been rendered 'to pass through the fire to Molech', with reference to children. What exactly does this mean? Does it refer to actual rites of human sacrifice or does it rather allude to less harmful acts of cultic dedication? Do rabbinic interpretations shed any light

(Amsterdam, 1700), ch. 8; J. G. Schwab, 'De Moloch et Remphan', D. Dietzsch, 'De cultu Molochi', and C. S. Ziegra, 'De crudelissima liberorum immolatione Molocho facta' in B. Ugolini (ed.), *Thesaurus Antiquitatum Sacrarum*, vol. 23 (Venice, 1760), pp. 631–44, 861–86, and 887–924; F. C. C. H. Münter, *Religion der Karthager*, 2nd edn (Copenhagen, 1821), pp. 5–61; F. C. Movers, *Die Phönizier*, vol. 1 (Bonn, 1841), pp. 322–498; G. F. Daumer, *Der Feuer- und Molochdienst der alten Hebräer* (Braunschweig, 1842); F. W. Ghillany (= R. von der Alm), *Die Menschenopfer der alten Hebräer* (Nürnberg, 1842); E. Meier, review of books by Daumer and Ghillany, *Theologische Studien und Kritiken* 16 (1843), 1007–53; A. Geiger, *Urschrift und Uebersetzungen der Bibel* (Breslau, 1857), pp. 299–308; H. Oort, *Het Menschenoffer in Israël* (Haarlem, 1865); A. Kuenen, 'Critische bijdragen tot de geschiedenis van den Israëlietischen godsdienst. I. De integriteit van Ex. XIII: 11–16', *Theologisch Tijdschrift* 1 (1867), 53–72, 'Critische bijdragen tot de geschiedenis van den Israëlietischen godsdienst. III. Jahveh en Moloch', *Theologisch Tijdschrift* 2 (1868), 559–98, *De Godsdienst van Israël*, vol. 1 (Haarlem, 1869), pp. 250–2 (ET, *The Religion of Israel*, vol. 1 [London, 1874], pp. 249–52); C. P. Tiele, *Vergelijkende Geschiedenis* (Amsterdam, 1872), pp. 457ff, 508ff, 692ff, *Geschiedenis van den Godsdienst in de Oudheid*, vol. 1 (Amsterdam, 1893), pp. 228f, 327ff; W. W. F. Graf von Baudissin, *Jahve et Moloch* (Leipzig, 1874), 'Moloch' in A. Hauck (ed.), *Realencyklopädie für protestantische Theologie und Kirche*, vol. 13, 3rd edn (Leipzig, 1903), pp. 269–303; P. Scholz, *Götzendienst und Zauberwesen* (Regensburg, 1877), pp. 182–217; B. D. Eerdmans, *Melekdienst en Vereering van Hemellichamen in Israël's Assyrische Periode* (Leiden, 1891); A. van Hoonacker, *Le Voeu de Jephté. Etude sur le chapitre XI du livre des Juges, suivie d'une notice sur Ezéchiel XX 25–26* (Louvain, 1893); A. H. H. Kamphausen, *Das Verhältnis des Menschenopfers zur israelitischen Religion* (Bonn, 1896); W. H. Bennett, 'Molech, Moloch' in J. Hastings (ed.), *A Dictionary of the Bible*, vol. 3 (Edinburgh, 1900), pp. 415–17; G. F. Moore, 'Biblical notes. 3. The image of Molech', *JBL* 16 (1897), 161–5, and 'Molech, Moloch', *Encyclopaedia Biblica*, vol. 3 (1902), cols. 3183–91; M.-J. Lagrange *Etudes sur les religions sémitiques*, 2nd edn (Paris, 1905), pp. 99–109; C. Mommert, *Menschenopfer bei den alten Hebräern* (Leipzig, 1905); E. Mader, *Die Menschenopfer der alten Hebräer und der benachbarten Völker* (Freiburg, 1909); P. Jensen, 'Alttestamentlich-Keilschriftliches. II. Die Götter כמוש und מֹלֶךְ und die Erscheinungsformen *Kammuš* und *Malik* des assyrisch-babylonischen Gottes *Nergal', Zeitschrift für Assyriologie 42,* NS8 (1934), 235–7. An important contribution to Molech studies was made by J. A. Montgomery, 'The holy city and Gehenna', *JBL* 27 (1908), 24–47, even though it was primarily concerned with the background to the concept of Gehenna. A useful survey of older research on Molech, from the seventeenth century down to Eissfeldt, may be found in Heider, *The Cult of Molek*, pp. 1–34. He has missed only a few of the studies listed above, e.g. the Dutch book by Eerdmans.

on the practice? The Molech cult, the nature of which will be discussed, had its centre in the valley of Hinnom by Jerusalem at a site called Topheth. What is the meaning of this word and is it, as some have claimed, an Aramaic loan-word?

This leads us to a further disputed question, namely the origin and background of the cult and the question who exactly Molech was (if we assume that this is the name of a god). Various Old Testament references tend to suggest a Canaanite origin, and sometimes Molech has been equated with the Canaanite god Baal. One may compare the fact that the Punic human sacrifices were dedicated to Baal-ḥammon, who I shall argue is indeed a form of Baal and not El, as is commonly supposed. Others see Molech as the Canaanite god Mot, or as a variant on the Ammonite god Milcom, or as equivalent to the Aramean Adad-milki. May there not have been a deity actually called *mlk*, however? If there is evidence for such a god, can anything be said about his character? And does the name Molech reflect the vowels of the Hebrew word *bōšeṯ* 'shame'? Whoever Molech was, some scholars have argued in spite of (or perhaps because of) the strength of the Old Testament's condemnation of Molech, that he was actually equated with Yahweh by those who practised his cult. Whether this was so will need to be considered, as will the question whether there was any connection between the sacrifices offered to Molech and the offering of the first-born to Yahweh. Various passages in the Old Testament where allusions to Molech have wrongly been detected will be examined, and after the final summary and conclusions, an appendix offers translations of the classical and patristic references to human sacrifice among the Phoenicians and Carthaginians.

1

Molech: divine name or sacrificial term?

Punic Molk sacrifices

Until 1935 it was universally believed that when the Old Testament speaks of Molech it is referring to a god. Scholars certainly differed on the question of the identity of the god and the nature of his cult, but there was nevertheless unanimous agreement that a god was intended. In 1935, Eissfeldt changed all this with the issue of a book with the bold title, *Molk als Opferbegriff im Punischen und Hebräischen und das Ende des Gottes Moloch*, which may be translated as 'Molk as sacrificial term in Punic and Hebrew and the end of the god Moloch'. In proclaiming the end of the god Molech, Eissfeldt proposed that the word *mōleḵ* was rather a term for a type of sacrifice, just as *mlk* (*molk*) in Punic is a sacrificial term. Although Eissfeldt's view of the nature of Molech in the Old Testament has proved very controversial – and this is something I shall discuss later – his opinion that *mlk* in Punic is a sacrificial term has been widely followed. However, even today there are still a few scholars who do not accept this view of the Punic data and prefer to translate *mlk* there as 'king', e.g. M. Weinfeld[1] and A. Cooper,[2] following the earlier lead of R. Charlier[3] and M. Buber.[4] Accordingly, before we can decide whether Eissfeldt's understanding of Molech in the Old Testament as a type of sacrifice is correct or not,

1 Cf. 'The worship of Molech and of the Queen of Heaven and its background', *UF* 4 (1972), 135–40.

2 'Divine names and epithets in the Ugaritic texts' in S. Rummel (ed.), *Ras Shamra Parallels*, vol. 3 (Rome, 1981), p. 446.

3 Cf. 'La nouvelle série de stèles puniques de Constantine et la question des sacrifices dits "molchomor", en relation avec l'expression "BŠRM BTM"', *Karthago* 4 (1953), 1–48; cf. previously, M. Lidzbarski, 'Neue Götter' in *Nachrichten von der königlichen Gesellschaft der Wissenschaften zu Göttingen* (Phil.-hist. Klasse, Heft 1, Göttingen, 1916), pp. 90f.

4 *Königtum Gottes*, 3rd edn (Heidelberg, 1956), p. 172 (ET, *Kingship of God* [London, 1967], pp. 178f).

it is necessary to determine whether the Punic word *mlk* bears this meaning.

As indicated above, a minority of scholars, including Charlier, Buber, and more recently Weinfeld and Cooper, have maintained that *mlk* is not the name of a sacrificial offering but is simply the word for 'king'. Thus, *mlk bʿl* would then mean 'king Baal' and *mlk ʾdm* 'king of mankind'. However, this view should be decisively rejected, as there are a number of places where this meaning is unsuitable, whereas the sacrificial interpretation makes excellent sense. For instance, there are occasions where *mlk* is mentioned after the name of the offerer rather than after the name of the god, for example:

lʿdn lbʿl ḥmn ndr ʾš nʿdr ʾdnbʿl bn ʿbdʾšmn mlk ʾdm bšrm bnʿ tm šmʿ qlʾ brkʾ

To the lord, to Baal-ḥammon, a vow which Adonbaal son of Abdeshmun vowed, an offering of a man, his own child, his son[5] in perfect condition. He heard his voice, he blessed him.[6]

The argument of Weinfeld[7] that the word order is insignificant as there are other variations in word order in the steles, is invalid, since in the present instance the placing of the words *mlk ʾdm* after the name of the offerer is inexplicable if they are an epithet of the god meaning 'king of mankind'. In keeping with the rendering 'offering of a man', it may be noted that there is abundant evidence of human sacrifice in the Punic world, not only from classical sources[8] but also from archaeological discoveries of cemeteries of sacrificed children (commonly referred to by scholars under the biblical name of 'topheth') at

5 For a discussion of the translation of *bšrm* see *KAI*, vol. 2, p. 97, and of *bnʿ tm* see *KAI*, vol. 2, p. 115. Also, on the translation of both expressions, cf. J. Hoftijzer, 'Eine Notiz zum punischen Kinderopfer', *VT* 8 (1958), 288–92.

6 *KAI*, 107 (=A. Berthier and R. Charlier, *Le Sanctuaire Punique d'El-Hofra à Constantine* [Paris, 1955], p. 35). Other examples of *mlk ʾdm* may be found in *RES* 334.3, 335.3, 336.2, and in Berthier and Charlier, *Le Sanctuaire Punique*, 28.1f, 29.1, 30.1f, 31.1, 32.2, 34.3f, 35.4, 36.2f, 37.2, 38.1f, 39.1, 40.3, 41.3. The translation 'an offering of a man' is the one most generally followed and seems to be correct. O. Eissfeldt, *Molk als Opferbegriff im Punischen und Hebräischen und das Ende des Gottes Moloch* (Halle, 1935), p. 19, preferred on balance to see a subjective genitive here, *ʾdm* referring to a layman (as opposed to a priest). However, the analogy of the expression *mlk ʾmr* 'an offering of a sheep' (cf. below, nn. 22–4) supports the common understanding of *mlk ʾdm* as involving an objective genitive. For convincing arguments against the view that *ʾdm* = blood (*dm* with prosthetic aleph), suggested by J. G. Février, 'Molchomor', *RHR* 143 (1953), 11, see Hoftijzer, 'Notiz zum punischen Kinderopfer', pp. 288ff.

7 'The worship of Molech', p. 138.

8 For translations of the classical sources, see below, pp. 87–91.

Motya (Mozia) in Sicily,[9] Monte Sirai,[10] Nora, Tharros and Sulcis[11] in Sardinia, and at Carthage, Sousse (Hadrumetum) and Cirta (near Constantine) in North Africa.[12]

Again, returning specifically to the translation of *mlk*, we find that *mlk* occurs in apposition to *mtnt*ʾ 'his gift', thus making it natural to render it as 'offering':

lʾdn lbʿl mtnt mtntʾ mlk bʿl ʾš ndr ʿzrbʿl bn bʿlḥnʾ bn bʿlytn ʾš bʿm ʾytnm

To the lord, to Baal a gift. His gift was an offering in place of a child,[13] which

9 Cf. A. Ciasca *et al.*, *Mozia*, vols. 1–9 (Rome, 1964–78); A. Ciasca, 'Mozia (Sicilia): il *tofet*. Campagne 1971–72', *RSF* 1 (1973), 94–8.

10 Cf. F. Barreca and G. Garbini, *Monte Sirai*, vol. 1 (Rome, 1964); M. G. Amadasi *et al.*, *Monte Sirai*, 2–4 (Rome, 1965–7); F. Barreca and S. F. Bondi, 'Scavi nel *tofet* di Monte Sirai, campagna 1979', *RSF*, 8 (1980), 143–5; P. Bartolini and S. F. Bondi, 'Monte Sirai 1980', *RSF*, 9 (1981), 216–30.

11 Cf. G. Pesce, *Sardegna punica* (Cagliari, 1961); S. Moscati, 'New Light on Punic Art' in W. A. Ward (ed.), *The Role of the Phoenicians in the Interaction of Mediterranean Civilizations* (Beirut, 1968), pp. 65–75; G. Chiera, *Testmonianze su Nora* (Collezione di studi fenici 11, Rome, 1978); P. Bartolini and C. Tronchetti, *La necropoli di Nora* (Collezione di studi fenici 12, Rome, 1981); E. Acquaro *et al.*, 'Tharros-I', *RSF* 3 (1975), 89–119, 'Tharros-II', *RSF* 3 (1975), 213–25, 'Tharros-III', *RSF* 4 (1976), 197–228; F. Fedele, 'Anthropologia fisica e paleocologia di Tharros: Nota preliminare sugli scavi del *tofet*, campagna 1976', *RSF* 5 (1977), 185–93; E. Acquaro *et al.*, 'Tharros-IV', *RSF* 6 (1978), 63–8, 'Tharros-V', *RSF* 7 (1979), 49–124, 'Tharros-VI', *RSF* 8 (1980), 79–142, 'Tharros-VII', *RSF* 9 (1981), 29–119, 'Tharros-VIII', *RSF* 10 (1982), 37–127, 'Tharros-IX', *RSF* 11 (1983), 49–111, 'Tharros-X', *RSF* 12 (1984), 47–101, 'Tharros-XI', *RSF* 13 (1985), 11–147, 'Tharros-XII', *RSF* 14 (1986), 95–107, 'Tharros-XIII', *RSF* 15 (1987), 75–9; S. Cecchini, 'Les stèles du tophet de Sulcis', *Actes du deuxième Congrès International d'études des Cultures de la Méditerranée Occidentale* (Algiers, 1978), 90–108; C. Tronchetti, 'Per la cronologia del tophet di S. Antico', *RSF* 7 (1979), 201–5.

12 Cf. L. Poinssot and R. Lantier, 'Un sanctuaire de Tanit à Carthage', *RHR* 44 (1923), 32–68; F. W. Kelsey, *Excavations at Carthage, 1925: A Preliminary Report* (New York, 1926); Berthier and Charlier, *Le Sanctuaire punique*; D. Harden, *The Phoenicians* (London, 1962), pp. 94–101; R. de Vaux, *Les Sacrifices de l'Ancien Testament* (Paris, 1964), pp. 69–76 (ET, *Studies in Old Testament Sacrifice* [Cardiff, 1964], pp. 75–84); S. Moscati, 'Il sacrificio dei fanciulli', *Rendiconti della Pontificia Accademia Romana di Archeologia* 38 (1965–6), 61–8, *The World of the Phoenicians* (ET, London, 1968), pp. 182–4, 192f, 198–201, and 'New light on Punic art' in Ward, *The Role of the Phoenicians*, pp. 65–75, and references; L. E. Stager, 'The rite of child sacrifice at Carthage' in J. G. Pedley (ed.), *New Light on Ancient Carthage* (Ann Arbor, 1980), pp. 1–11, and 'Carthage: a view from the Tophet' in H. G. Niemeyer (ed.), *Phönizier im Westen* (Madrider Beiträge 8, Mainz, 1982), pp. 155–66; and for a popular presentation see L. E. Stager and S. R. Wolff, 'Child sacrifice at Carthage – religious rite or population control?', *BARev* 10, no. 1 (Jan./Feb., 1984), 31–51. It may also be noted that a stele from Carthage depicts a priest carrying a child in his arms exactly as other priests carry their animal victim. Cf. G. Charles-Picard, *Les Religions de l'Afrique antique* (Paris, 1954), p. 45, fig. 4.

13 'Offering in place of a child' would seem to be the most commonly accepted rendering of *mlk bʿl*, the second word being analysed as b^e + *ʿūl* 'child' (cf. Hebrew *ʿūl* 'child, suckling'). Cf. Février, 'Molchomor', p. 16 and 'Essai de reconstruction

Azrubaal, son of Baalḥanno, son of Baalyaton had vowed, who belongs to the people of *ʾytnm*.[14]

Finally, it may be noted that, besides the form *mlk*, we also find the feminine form *mlkt* occurring before *bʿl*. To translate 'queen Baal' would be nonsensical, and 'queen of Baal' is not possible, since the stele in question explicitly states that the deity involved is simply Baal-ḥammon:

nṣb mlkt bʿl ʾš pʿl bdsy bn mlqrtgd lbʿl ḥmn ʾdn

Stele of the offering in place of a child, which Bodisi son of Melqartgad made to Baal-ḥammon the lord.[15]

The form *mlkt* also occurs in one other Punic inscription, where again it is inappropriate to translate it as 'queen':

lrbt ltnt pn bʿl wlʾdn lbʿl ḥmn ʾš ndr mgn ʿl ʾdnbʿl nṣb mlkt bmṣrm

To the lady, to Tinnit face of Baal, and to the lord, to Baal-ḥammon, which Magon vowed concerning Adonbaal, stele of an offering in distress.[16]

It may therefore be concluded that Eissfeldt and the majority of scholars are right in maintaining that *mlk* in the Punic inscriptions refers to a kind of sacrificial offering. However, the word should not be related to Syriac *m^elak̲* 'to promise', as Eissfeldt (following Chabot) believed,[17] since the *mlk* clearly refers to the sacrifice itself,

du sacrifice molek', *JA* 248 (1960), 177; *KAI*, vol. 2, p. 76. This rendering, however, is not certain. Nevertheless, it does seem preferable to other proposals made so far. J. C. L. Gibson's claim in *Textbook of Syrian Semitic Inscriptions*, vol. 3 (Oxford, 1982), p. 75, that the translation 'in place of a child' is based on a misunderstanding of the *beth pretii*, which would mean 'at the cost of' rather than 'in place of', probably rests on an artificial distinction (at least in origin); cf. D. Pardee, 'The preposition in Ugaritic', *UF* 8 (1976), 299f, and C. H. Gordon, '"In" of predication or equivalence', *JBL* 100 (1981), 613, for two slightly different views. Moreover, Gibson's own rendering, *Textbook*, pp. 74f, 'a (human) sacrifice of one making (it)', based on E. Lipiński's proposed 'Votivopfer des Spenders' ('votive offering of the giver') in W. Beyerlin (ed.), *Religionsgeschichtliches Textbuch zum Alten Testament* (Göttingen, 1975), p. 252 (ET, *Near Eastern Religious Texts Relating to the Old Testament* [London, 1978], pp. 234f), appears a little awkward. The other proposal to render *mlk bʿl* as 'offering of a citizen', adopted by F. Rosenthal in *ANET*, p. 658, and also P. G. Mosca, 'Child Sacrifice in Canaanite and Israelite Religion: A study in Mulk and Molech' (unpublished Ph.D thesis, Harvard University, 1975), and Stager and Wolff, 'Child sacrifice at Carthage', pp. 45f, is also open to question. This rendering clearly understands *bʿl* as subjective genitive (for an objective 'infant citizen' would be unlikely), but the analogy of *mlk ʾmr* would make an objective genitive preferable, if *bʿl* really were simply a noun here.

14 *KAI* 99. 15 *CIS* 1, 5684. 16 *Ibid*., 198.

17 *Molk als Opferbegriff*, p. 4, following J.-B. Chabot, 'Note complémentaire de M. J.-B. Chabot', *CRAIBL* (1931), 27.

not the promise of it. Rather, it should be regarded as a peformative-*m* noun from the root *hlk* 'to go', as W. von Soden[18] first argued. A. Alt[19] pointed out in support that the *yiphʿil* of *hlk* occurs in Phoenician at Karatepe with the meaning 'to offer up (of sacrifice)' (*KAI* 26A.II.19, *wylk zbḥ*, cf. C.IV.2).[20] *Mlk* is then comparable to other sacrificial terms derived from verbs of motion, e.g. Hebrew *ʿōlāh*, *qorbān* and Akkadian *muḫḫuru*.

It would seem, therefore, that the word *mlk* simply means 'offering'. This is agreed by Eissfeldt. It does not, as sometimes appears to be imagined, mean specifically 'human sacrifice'.[21] *Mlk ʾdm* certainly means 'human sacrifice' (lit. 'sacrifice of a man'), but *ʾdm* needs to be added to give it this meaning. That *mlk* of itself cannot mean 'human sacrifice' is shown by the expression *mlk ʾmr* 'sacrifice of a sheep'.[22] Even though the sheep could be a substitute for a man, this does not make *mlk* itself a word for 'human sacrifice'. That *ʾmr* is here the word for sheep is widely accepted, and is supported by the fact that Latin steles from Ngaous (formerly Nicivibus) in Algeria (*c.* A.D. 200)[23] containing the expression *molchomor* (i.e. Punic *mlk ʾmr*

18 Review of Eissfeldt in *ThLZ* 61 (1936), col. 46.

19 'Die phönikischen Inschriften von Karatepe', *Die Welt des Orients* 1 (1949), 282f.

20 Février, 'Molchomor', p. 8, also compares Num. 17.11 (ET 16.46), where the *hiphʿil* of *hlk* occurs with the meaning 'bring' in a cultic context.

21 E.g. Gibson, *Textbook*, vol. 3, pp. 74–6. Cf. *NEB* margin to Lev. 20.5, which renders Hebrew *mōleḵ* as 'human sacrifice', thereby presupposing this meaning for Punic *mlk*.

22 Occurrences of the expression *mlk ʾmr* include Berthier and Charlier, *Le Sanctuaire Punique*, 55.1f, and *CIS* 1, 307.4f. It is probable that we should read *mlk ʾmr* rather than *mlk ʾsr* in *CIS* 1, 123, *bis* 1f (cf. R. Dussaud, 'Précisions épigraphiques touchant les sacrifices puniques d'enfants', *CRAIBL* [1946], 376ff). In Berthier and Charlier, *Le Sanctuaire Punique*, 54.2f, we find the variant *mlʾk ʾmr*, while in 56.1, *mlk ʾtr* appears to be a mistake for *mlk ʾmr* (cf. *ibid.*, p. 51).

23 Two types of dedication are found in these steles, the former in stele no. 1 and the latter in steles nos. 2–4. The former reads:

Quod bonum et faustum feliciter sit factum domino sancto Saturno sacrum magnum nocturnum morchomor ex voto Aquilius Victor et Aelia Rufina coniux eius pro imperato eius audito.

'Prosperity, salvation and happiness! To the holy lord Saturn a great nocturnal sacrifice *morchomor* on account of a vow of Aquilius Victor and his wife Aelia Rufina in obedience to his command.' The second type of dedication, as witnessed by stele no. 3, the best preserved of steles nos. 2–4, runs as follows:

Quod bonum et faustum sit domino sancto Saturno magnum nocturnum anima pro anima sanguine pro sanguine vita pro vita Concessae salute ex viso et voto sacrum reddiderunt molchomor Felix et Diodora libentes animo agnum pro vikario.

Prosperity and salvation! To the holy lord Saturn a great nocturnal sacrifice – breath for breath, blood for blood, life for life, for the salvation of Concessa – on account of a vision and a vow Felix and Diodora have offered a sacrifice *molchomor* with willing hearts, a lamb as substitute.' (Cf. Eissfeldt, *Molk als Opferbegriff*, pp. 3–4 and pl. I)

in Latin transcription), actually contain carvings of a ram on them and indicate the nature of the sacrifice by the phrase *agnum pro vikario* 'a lamb as substitute'.[24] In conclusion, therefore, *mlk* of itself cannot mean 'human sacrifice'; rather it is a general word used for 'sacrifice', the nature of which is indicated by an accompanying word.

Eissfeldt's view of Molech as a sacrificial term in the Old Testament

We have seen above that there can be now not the slightest doubt that *molk* (*mlk*) is a sacrificial term in the Punic texts. Is this the case, however, in the Old Testament, as Eissfeldt and a number of other scholars have believed,[25] or should we continue to find allusions there to a divine name or title Molech?[26] It is true that one may feel tempted to see Hebrew *mōleḵ* as a comparable sacrificial term to Punic *molk*

24 For these reasons the rendering of *mlk ʾmr* as 'offering of a sheep' has rightly been widely accepted. The objection of Lipiński, 'Votivopfer' in Beyerlin (ed.), *Religionsgeschichtliches Textbuch*, p. 252 (ET, *Near Eastern Religious Texts*, p. 234) and Gibson, *Textbook*, vol. 3, pp. 76f, that the Latin transcription *-omor* does not correspond very well with the vocalization of Punic *ʾmr* but presupposes rather a participle of the verb *ʾmr* 'to say, promise' is not compelling. The vocalization *-omor* does not correspond exactly with one of the participles either (*ʾōmēr, ʾāmūr*). Moreover, it is perfectly conceivable that an original *a* vowel in the second half of the word for sheep (cf. Aramaic *ʾimmar* or *ʾīmmar*) developed into an *o* through the process *a→ā→o*, and the vowel in the first half of the word could have become an *o* through attraction to it.

25 Eissfeldt, *Molk als Opferbegriff*. pp. 36–44. Eissfeldt's view has been followed by a number of scholars including R. Dussaud, review of Eissfeldt, *Syria* 16 (1935), 407–9, and *Les Origines cananéennes du sacrifice israélite*, 2nd edn (Paris, 1941), pp. 352–4 (but cf. his review of Eissfeldt in *Archiv für Orientforschung* 11 [1936], 167f, where he concedes that in *some* places the redactors have made Molech a god, e.g. Lev. 20.5); von Soden, review of Eissfeldt, *ThLZ* 61 (1936), cols. 45f; W. J. Harrelson, 'Molech, Moloch' in H. H. Rowley and F. C. Grant (eds.), *Dictionary of the Bible*, 2nd edn of work originally edited by J. Hastings (Edinburgh, 1963), p. 669; A. R. Johnson, *Sacral Kingship in Ancient Israel*, 2nd edn (Cardiff, 1967), p. 45, n. 4, finds Eissfeldt's argument 'attractive and, on the whole, convincing'; H. H. Rowley, *Dictionary of Bible Themes* (London, 1968), p. 63, is uncertain but thinks Eissfeldt's view is more likely than that Molech is a god's name; W. F. Albright, *Yahweh and the Gods of Canaan* (London, 1968), pp. 205f (though cf. his book *Archaeology and the Religion of Israel*, 5th edn [Garden City, 1969], pp. 156–8, for a more nuanced presentation of his view); Gibson, *Textbook*, vol. 3, p. 75, finds no clear statements in the Punic texts as to the meaning of *mlk* but thinks that the biblical references support the view that it is a term for human sacrifice; Stager and Wolff, 'Child sacrifice at Carthage', p. 47. Eissfeldt's view is also taken up and developed in Mosca, 'Child sacrifice in Canaanite and Israelite religion'.

26 Among those rejecting Eissfeldt's thesis are the following: A. Bea, 'Kinderopfer für Moloch oder für Jahwe?', *Biblica* 18 (1937), 95–107; A. Jirku, 'Gab es im Alten Testament einen Gott Molek (Melek)?', *Archiv für Religionswissenschaft* 35 (1938), 178–9; W. Kornfeld, 'Der Moloch. Eine Untersuchung zur Theorie O. Eissfeldts', *Wiener Zeitschrift für die Kunde des Morgenlandes* 51 (1952), 287–313; K.

on the grounds that the common context of human sacrifice of Canaanite origin that both reflect makes it seem improbable that there is no connection between them. Further, as Eissfeldt pointed out, the rendering of *l^{e}mōleḵ* by 'as a *molk* sacrifice' is linguistically conceivable, in the light of comparable examples of *l^{e}* + sacrificial term, as in *l^{e}ʿōlāh* 'as a burnt offering' (Gen. 22.2, 13), *l^{e}ʾāšām* 'as a guilt offering', and *l^{e}ḵol neḏer* 'for any vow' (Deut. 23.19, ET 18).[27] However, there are a number of points to be made against Eissfeldt's view, which make it clear that the sacrificial interpretation is to be rejected.

(i) As has frequently been pointed out,[28] Eissfeldt's interpretation of Lev. 20.5 is forced. The Hebrew text (*w^{e}ʾēṯ kol-hazzōnīm ʾaḥ^{a}rāyw liz^{e}nōṯ ʾaḥ^{a}rē hammōleḵ*) is commonly rendered, 'all who follow him in playing the harlot after Molech', but on Eissfeldt's interpretation this reads 'all who follow him in playing the harlot after a *molk* sacrifice'. This is clearly unacceptable in the light of the numerous references elsewhere in the Old Testament to the Israelites playing the harlot after pagan deities, e.g. Exod. 34.15, 16; Lev. 17.7; Deut. 31.16; Judg. 2.17, 8.33; 1 Chron. 5.25; 2 Chron. 21.11, 13; Ps. 106.39; Isa. 57.3; Jer. 3.1, 2, 6, 8–9; Ezek. 6.9, 16.15, 16, 17, 26, 28, 30, 31, 33, 34, 35, 41, 20.30, 23.3, 5, 19, 43, 44; Hos. 1.2, 2.7 (ET 5), 4.12, 5.3; Mic. 1.7. On the other hand, nowhere else do we find an allusion to the Israelites playing the harlot after a sacrifice. It is true that Eissfeldt seeks to minimize the effect of this criticism by appealing to the very next verse of Leviticus, Lev. 20.6, where we read of people playing the harlot after ghosts and spirits, and also to Judg. 8.27, where Israel plays the harlot after Gideon's ephod. With regard to the former passage, it may be said that the notion of playing the harlot after ghosts and spirits represents a legitimate extension of the concept of playing the harlot after gods, since ghosts and spirits are twice spoken of in the Old Testament as gods (cf. 1 Sam. 28.13; Isa. 8.19).[29] As for playing the harlot after the ephod in Judg. 8.27, we are here faced with

Dronkert, *De Molochdienst in het Oude Testament* (Leiden, 1953); E. Dhorme, 'Le dieu Baal et le dieu Moloch dans la tradition biblique', *Anatolian Studies* 6 (1956), 57–61; J. Gray, *The Legacy of Canaan*, 2nd edn, *SVT* 5 (1965), 172, n.2; W. Zimmerli, *Ezechiel*, vol. 1 (Neukirchen-Vluyn, 1969), p. 357 (ET, *Ezekiel*, vol. 1 [Philadelphia, 1979], p. 344); G. C. Heider, *The Cult of Molek: A Reassessment* (Sheffield, 1985).

27 Cf. Eissfeldt, *Molk als Opferbegriff*, p. 38.

28 E.g. Bea, 'Kinderopfer', p. 100; Jirku, 'Gott Molek', p. 179; Kornfeld, 'Der Moloch', pp. 300f; Heider, *The Cult of Molek*, pp. 233–52.

29 In Isa. 8.19 I render *ʾ^{e}lōhāyw* as 'their gods' with most commentators, rather than 'their God'. Cf. parallelism with *hammēṯīm* 'the dead'.

the problem of exactly what the ephod was.[30] It serves in the P Code as an elaborate High Priestly garment to which the breastplate containing the Urim and Thummim was attached (cf. Exod. 28. 39). In earlier sources the ephod sometimes appears as a simpler priestly garment, a loin cloth made of linen (cf. 1 Sam. 2.18; 2 Sam. 6.14), and sometimes as an object in the possession of the priests employed in obtaining oracles from Yahweh (1 Sam. 23.6, 9, 30.7, cf. 1 Sam. 2.28, 14.3, 21.10, ET 9, 22.18). Whether the latter two are to be equated is a subject of dispute, but in my view it is simpler to do so. In any case it is clear that there was an oracular ephod and it appears that it was associated with the sacred lots Urim and Thummim (cf. 1 Sam. 14.3, 41) just as we later find in the P Code (cf. Exod. 28). It is this oracular ephod to which Judg. 8.27 presumably alludes. It is therefore interesting to note that Hos. 4.12 likewise employs the imagery of playing the harlot in connection with seeking oracles: 'My people inquire of a thing of wood, and their staff gives them oracles. For a spirit of harlotry has led them astray, and they have left their God to play the harlot.'

To return to Eissfeldt, it may be concluded that there is sufficient similarity between seeking after pagan gods and seeking after false divine oracles for one to understand how the imagery of playing the harlot could easily be extended from the one to the other, but the idea of playing the harlot after a sacrifice would be quite different and totally unparalleled. Finally in this connection it may be noted that a further point supporting the view that it is a god Molech and not a

30 Cf. T. C. Foote, 'The ephod', *JBL* 21 (1902), 1–47; E. Sellin, 'Das israelitische Ephod' in C. Bezold (ed.), *Orientalische Studien Theodor Nöldeke zum siebzigsten Geburtstag*, vol. 2 (Giessen, 1906), pp. 699–717; W. R. Arnold, *Ephod and Ark* (Cambridge, Mass., 1917); J. Gabriel, *Untersuchungen über das alttestamentliche Priestertum, mit besonderer Berücksichtigung des hohenpriesterlichen Ornates* (Vienna, 1933), pp. 44–70; E. Sellin, 'Ephod und Terafim', *JPOS* 14 (1934), 185–94; H. Thiersch, *Ependytes und Ephod. Gottesbild und Priesterkleid im alten Vorderasien* (Stuttgart, 1936); E. Sellin, 'Zu Efod und Terafim', *ZAW* 55 (1937), 296–8, and 'Noch einmal der alttestamentliche Efod', *JPOS* 17 (1937), 236–51; H. G. May, 'Ephod and Ariel', *AJSL* 56 (1939), 44–52; W. F. Albright, 'Are the ephod and the teraphim mentioned in Ugaritic literature?', *BASOR* 83 (1941), 39–42; J. Morgenstern, 'The Ark, the Ephod and the Tent of Meeting', *HUCA* 18 (1943–4), 1–17; M. Haran, צורת האפוד במקורות המקראיים, *Tarbiz* 24 (1955), 380–91 (English summary on pp. II–III); K. Elliger, 'Ephod und Choschen', *VT* 8 (1958), 19–35; R. de Vaux, *Les Institutions de l'Ancien Testament*, vol. 2 (Paris, 1960), pp. 201–4 (ET, *Ancient Israel*, 2nd edn [London, 1965], pp. 349–52); J. Lindblom, 'Lot-casting in the Old Testament', *VT* 12 (1962), 164–78); A. Phillips, 'David's linen ephod', *VT* 19 (1969), 485–7; N. L. Tidwell, 'The linen ephod: 1 Sam. II 18 and 2 Sam. VI 14', *VT* 24 (1974), pp. 505–7; P. R. Davies, 'Ark or ephod in 1 Sam. XIV. 18?', *JTS* 26 NS (1975), 82–7.

sacrificial *molk* after which people play the harlot in Lev. 20.5 is that the same harlotry language is applied to the god, not the sacrifice, in the following passage having to do with human sacrifice, in which the Molech cult is probably included: Ezek. 23.37: 'For they have committed adultery, and blood is upon their hands; with their idols they have committed adultery; and they have even offered up to them for food the sons whom they had borne to me.' (Cf. too Ps. 106.37–9.)

(ii) Not only *znh* 'to play the harlot', but other verbs associated with the Molech cult, give strong support to the view that Molech is a god and not a sacrifice, i.e. the verbs *ʿbr* (in the *hiphʿil*) 'to offer up, devote', *ntn* 'to give', and *śrp* 'to burn'. None of these verbs ever occurs with *l*^{e} + sacrificial term alone, but they are well attested with *l*^{e} + divine name. Thus compare Exod. 13.12, 'you shall devote to the Lord all that first opens the womb' (*w*^{e}*ha*^{ʿa}*ḇartā . . . laYHWH*) and Ezek. 16.21, 'that you slaughtered my children and delivered them up as an offering to them?' (*b*^{e} *ha*^{ʿa}*ḇīr . . . lāhem*). A further passage is Ezek. 23.37, 'and they have even offered up to them for food (*he*^{ʿe}*ḇīrū lāhem l*^{e}*ʾoḵlāh*) the sons whom they had borne to me'. Although in this one instance we do find the verb *ʿbr* + *l*^{e} + sacrificial term, the latter does not stand alone but contains likewise *l*^{e} + divinities (*lāhem*). It is therefore not an exception to the rule noted above. Similarly *śrp* 'to burn' is likewise found with *l*^{e} + divine name but never with *l*^{e} + sacrificial term (though there is one isolated case of *ntn* with *l*^{e} + sacrificial term, in 1 Chron. 21.23).

(iii) It is surprising that there is no recollection of a sacrificial meaning of *mōleḵ* in any of the ancient Versions if the word had indeed borne this meaning.[31] That some of the Versions should have failed to detect the meaning some of the time would be understandable, but that all the Versions should misconstrue the meaning all the time would be improbable.

In conclusion, then, it may be stated that there are no compelling

31 The renderings of MT Molech in the main ancient Versions may here be noted. The LXX translates *ἄρχοντι* in Lev. 18.21, 20.2, 3, 4, *ἄρχοντας* in Lev. 20.5, *βασιλεῖ αὐτῶν* in 1 Kgs 11.7, *Μολοχ* in 2 Kings 23.10, and *Μολοχ βασιλεῖ* in Jer. 32 (39). 35. The renderings of Aquila, Symmachus and Theodotion are not recorded for all instances, but where they occur we find *Μολοχ*. The Vulgate consistently renders *Moloch* in all cases. When we come to the Targums we find that, in Leviticus, Targum Onqelos transliterates the word (*mwlk*), Targum Pseudo-Jonathan has *pūlḥānā nūḵrāʾāh*, except Lev. 20.2, where it transliterates (*mwlk*), and Targum Neofiti 1 has *polḥānāh noḵrīyyāh*. In 1 Kgs. 11.7, 2 Kgs. 23.10, and Jer. 32.35, Targum Jonathan transliterates (*mwlk*). The Peshiṭta has *nuḵrāyṯā* in all the Leviticus verses, *malkōm* in 1 Kgs. 11.7, and *ʾamleḵ* in 2 Kgs. 23.10 and Jer. 32.35.

reasons for supposing that *mōlek̲* in the Old Testament should be equated with Punic *molk*.

An examination of the view that Molech was originally a sacrificial term but was misunderstood by the Old Testament as a divine name

Granted that Eissfeldt was wrong in seeing *mōlek̲* in the Old Testament as a sacrificial term rather than a divine name or title, may it nevertheless not be the case that the word *molk* 'sacrificial offering' lies behind the Old Testament references, but that it was misunderstood by the Old Testament writers, who mistakenly took it to be a divine name or title? A number of scholars have adopted this view, including Cazelles and de Vaux.[32] One can understand the attraction of this standpoint, since it enables one to accept the natural meaning of *mōlek̲* as a divine name, whilst at the same time maintaining that it is not simply coincidence that the same word is used in human sacrificial contexts in both Punic texts and the Old Testament.

However, in spite of its superficial attractiveness, this view is in all probability to be rejected, for the following reasons:

(i) If the Old Testament has misunderstood the term *mōlek̲*, it has done so not once, but consistently, in the works of various writers, including the Holiness Code, the Deuteronomistic history, the Deuteronomistic redaction of Jeremiah, Trito-Isaiah and perhaps the prophet Zephaniah.[33] Although it is conceivable that one writer might have misunderstood the expression, it would be remarkable if all of them had done so, especially since they wrote at the time when, and in several cases the place where, the cult was being practised. It is surely more scientific to accept the testimony of these first-hand sources, whose authors were well placed to know the facts, than to suppose that we are in a position to overturn this evidence on the basis of Punic texts written in a different part of the world.[34]

32 H. Cazelles, 'Molok' in L. Pirot, A. Robert and H. Cazelles (eds.), *Dictionnaire de la Bible Supplément*, vol. 5 (Paris, 1957), cols. 1337–46; de Vaux, *Les Sacrifices*, pp. 79–81 (ET, *Studies in Old Testament Sacrifice*, pp. 87–90). It should be noted that this represents a development in de Vaux's view, since in his earlier review of Eissfeldt's book in *RB* 45 (1936), 278–82, he saw Hebrew *mōlek̲* as simply a divine name without connection with the Punic sacrificial term *molk*.

33 On Zeph. 1.5, cf. below, p. 69.

34 On the other hand, we may not legitimately criticize the comparison of the Punic texts on the basis of their later date, *contra* M. J. Mulder, *Kanaänitische goden in het Oude Testament* (The Hague, 1965), p. 61, since, as a matter of fact, although most of them are much later, *mlk* is already attested as a sacrificial term in a Punic text

(ii) It is perhaps conceivable that a rare word confined to a specific context of human sacrifice might have been misunderstood as the name of the deity to whom the sacrifice was offered. However, as we have noted earlier,[35] the word *molk* in Punic does not of itself mean 'human sacrifice' but is a general word meaning 'sacrificial offering'. If the word existed in the language of Palestine – something which still remains unproved – then similarly there we should expect it to have been a term denoting sacrificial offerings generally. Such a word would therefore not have been confined to the specific context of human sacrifice, and it would be surprising that a word of such general usage should have been so radically misunderstood.

(iii) As we shall see later in this monograph, there was in fact a god named *mlk* or Molech.[36] Moreover, as will also emerge, there are good reasons for assigning him an underworld role, which agrees well with the evidence of the Old Testament, e.g. Isa. 57.9. It is therefore perverse to suppose that the Old Testament is not alluding to this deity but has rather misunderstood a sacrificial term.

from Malta from the seventh or sixth century B.C. Cf. O. Eissfeldt, 'The beginnings of Phoenician epigraphy according to a letter written by Wilhelm Gesenius in 1835', *PEQ* 79 (1947), 85f.

35 Cf. above, pp. 4–9, esp. pp. 8f.

36 Cf. below, pp. 46–50.

2
The nature of the Molech cult and the meaning of Topheth

The nature of the Molech cult: human sacrifice or cultic dedication?

The nature of the Molech cult is a question which is still a subject of considerable dispute, a dispute going back even to the pre-critical era. On the one hand there are those who see it in terms of human sacrifice, whilst on the other hand there are those who claim that this is a misunderstanding and that nothing more than cultic dedication was involved, possibly even including a sexual element. Those who reject the sacrificial interpretation, however, differ in whether they hold that the Old Testament itself (wrongly) associates human sacrifice with the Molech cult or not. In the present section I shall examine the questions involved in this matter in an attempt to discover where the truth lies.

A characteristic expression used in connection with the Molech cult is *hʿbyr bʾš*, which has traditionally been rendered 'to cause to pass through the fire'. It is employed explicitly of the Molech cult in 2 Kgs. 23.10, and it is likely that it is to this cult that the expression is applied in 2 Kgs. 16.3, 21.6 and 2 Chron. 33.6, whilst it is employed in a broader connection, surely including the Molech cult, in Deut. 18.10 and Ezek. 20.31.[1] We also find *hʿbyr* used alone without *bʾš* in connection with the Molech cult explicitly in Lev. 18.21 and Jer. 32.35, and there can be little doubt that its occurrence in Ezek. 16.21, 23.37 refers partly to this cult. The question therefore arises whether it is human sacrifice or some more harmless ritual which is involved in these passages. There can be no doubt that the Old Testament itself understands the terms in the sacrificial sense. Thus, from the passages listed above this is made clear in Ezek. 16.21, 'that you slaughtered

1 *Hʿbyr bʾš* also occurs in 2 Kgs. 17.17 in connection with the Northern Kingdom. It is not impossible that the Molech cult is intended here, but it has to be noted that elsewhere in the Old Testament the Molech cult is associated only with Jerusalem.

(*wattišḥ^{a}ṭī*) my children and delivered them up to be offered to them', and in Ezek. 23.37, 'For they have committed adultery, and blood is upon their hands; with their idols they have committed adultery; and they have even offered up to them for food (*l^{e}'oḵlāh*) the sons whom they had borne to me'. Two verses on, in Ezek. 23.39 we also read: 'For when they had slaughtered (*ūḇ^{e}šaḥ^{a}ṭām*) their children to their idols, on the same day they came into my sanctuary to profane it. And lo, this is what they did in my house.' Although the Molech cult is not explicitly mentioned here, it is probably included in the references to human sacrifice. In any case, it clearly indicates the way in which the verb *hʿbyr* was interpreted, a verb used where Molech is explicitly mentioned and whose meaning is the subject of the present discussion. Another passage where the verb 'slaughter' (*šḥṭ*) is used is Isa. 57.5, where the prophet declares, 'you who burn with lust among the oaks, under every luxuriant tree; who slay (*šōḥ^{a}ṭē*) your children in the valleys, under the clefts of the rocks'.[2] Now it is striking that just four verses later, in verse 9, Molech is actually mentioned: 'You journeyed to Molech[3] with oil and multiplied your perfumes; you sent your envoys far off, and sent down even to Sheol.' It is attractive to suppose that verses 5 and 9 are speaking about the same thing, the cult of human sacrifice in honour of the god Molech. Indeed, the words, 'you sent your envoys far off, and sent down even to Sheol', may well be a poetic way of referring to the fate of the children being sent to death for Molech. This suggestion further gains in plausibility when we note the association of oil and unguents in connection with Molech in Isa. 57.9, which may be compared with Ezek. 16.18f, which mentions oil, incense, honey and also flour in close association with human sacrifice (Ezek. 16.20f).

One of the passages listed above where *hʿbyr* is explicitly mentioned in connection with Molech is Jer. 32.35, where we read: 'They built the high places of Baal in the valley of the son of Hinnom, to offer up their sons and daughters to Molech, though I did not command them, nor did it enter into my mind, that they should do

2 J. C. Greenfield, 'The prepositions b ..... taḥat in Jes 57 5', *ZAW* 73 (1961), 226–8, argues that *taḥaṯ* is capable of meaning 'among' as well as 'under', and translates here '... who slay their children in the valleys, *among* the clefts of the rocks'. He thinks that the reference is to 'clefts in the rock in which a person can hide out or carry out a foul act rather than overhanging cliffs' (*ibid.*, p. 228, n. 13). This translation is not impossible but there seem no compelling reasons for abandoning the more usual meaning of *taḥaṯ* here (attested, e.g., in the parallel line in v. 5a), since the fact that the action occurs in a valley makes a reference to its taking place *under* clefts of the rocks seem entirely appropriate.

3 MT *meleḵ*. Cf. below, pp. 50–2.

this abomination, to cause Judah to sin.' There are two other passages in the prose material in the book of Jeremiah which are almost identical with Jer. 32.35 in wording and refer to the same Hinnom valley cult (though Molech is not explicitly named) in which the verb used is *śrp* 'to burn', which makes it abundantly clear that real burning was involved. The first passage is Jer. 7.31, 'And they have built the high place[4] of Topheth, which is in the valley of the son of Hinnom, to burn their sons and daughters in the fire, which I did not command, nor did it come into my mind', and the second is Jer. 19.5, 'and they have built the high places of Baal to burn their sons in the fire,[5] which I did not command, nor did it come into my mind'.

Again there is a passage in Isa. 30.33 which also clearly implies that the Molech cult involved burning to the point of destruction, but its relevance to the particular question under discussion has never previously been noted, as far as I am aware. This verse is unique in the Old Testament in that it is not speaking of the Molech cult directly, but rather employs the language of the cult (*topteh*, a variant of *tōpet*; *lammelek*)[6] to describe the coming destruction of the Assyrians: 'For the oven (*topteh*) has long been prepared, yea for the king (*lammelek*) it is made ready, its pyre made deep and wide,[7] with fire and wood in abundance; the breath of the Lord, like a stream of brimstone, kindles it.' The importance of this passage lies in the fact that it is set in a context speaking of the total destruction of the Assyrians (cf. vv. 30ff). This verse therefore confirms the sacrificial understanding of the Molech cult and is inconsistent with the view that merely dedication was involved.

Faced with this clear testimony from the Old Testament that the Molech cult involved human sacrifice and real burning, how do those

4 Reading the singular with the LXX and Targum. The MT has the plural 'high places'.

5 Omitting the words *ʿōlōt labbāʿal* 'as burnt offerings to Baal' with the LXX. It is widely accepted that the LXX represents an earlier form of the text of Jeremiah than the MT. Cf. J. G. Janzen, *Studies in the Text of Jeremiah* (Cambridge, Mass., 1973); E. Tov, 'L'incidence de la critique textuelle sur la critique littéraire dans le livre de Jérémie', *RB* 79 (1972), 189–99.

6 Contrary to the majority opinion among scholars, G. C. Heider, *The Cult of Molek: A Reassessment* (Sheffield, 1985), pp. 322f, does not see *lammelek* as referring to Molech or the divine king, but rather to the Assyrian king. However, this seems unlikely in view of the evident meaning of *lammōlek* (associated with *tōpet*) elsewhere. Heider fully recognizes that imagery from the Molech cult is being employed here, but he fails to observe the support that this passage gives to the sacrificial interpretation. In general, however, Heider has marshalled the evidence well in support of the sacrificial understanding of the Molech cult.

7 Reading *haʿmēq harḥēb* for MT *heʿmīq hirḥib*, cf. Targum.

scholars who think simply in terms of cultic dedication deal with this evidence? Some, such as N. H. Snaith and D. Plataroti,[8] do not seem to be aware of it, since they claim that the Old Testament itself gives no support to the sacrificial interpretation. This will clearly not do. Others, however, such as Weinfeld[9] admit that the Old Testament itself indicates that the Molech cult involved human sacrifice – though they are not aware of the probable implication of Isa. 57.9 and the certain implication of Isa. 30.33 – but claim that the Old Testament is exaggerating. R. P. Carroll,[10] for example, claims that 'propagandist abuse is seldom accurate', but such a generalized statement hardly counts as an argument when we recall that we have independent confirmation of human sacrifice in the Canaanite world (Carthaginian and Phoenician) from many classical sources, Punic inscriptions and archaeological evidence, as well as Egyptian depictions of the ritual taking place in Syria/Palestine.[11] Again, T. H. Gaster and Weinfeld[12] appeal to a custom attested in various parts of the world in which passing between rows of fire served as a means of purification and dedication. However, it is difficult to understand the scholarly principle involved in preferring alleged far-flung anthropological parallels to the evidence of the biblical text itself. Weinfeld[13]

8 N. H. Snaith, 'The cult of Molech', *VT* 16 (1966), 123–4; D. Plataroti, 'Zum Gebrauch des Wortes *mlk* im Alten Testament', *VT* 28 (1978), 286–300.

9 'The worship of Molech and of the Queen of Heaven and its background', *UF* 4 (1972), 140–1.

10 R. P. Carroll, *From Chaos to Covenant* (London, 1981), p. 304.

11 For classical citations see below, pp. 86–91, for Punic texts see above, pp. 4–9, and for archaeological evidence see above, pp. 5–6 with nn. 9–12. For Egyptian depictions of the ritual of human sacrifice in Syria/Palestine, see P. Derchain, 'Les plus anciens témoignages de sacrifices d'enfants chez les Sémites occidentaux', *VT* 20 (1970), 351–5; O. Keel, 'Kanaanäische Sühneriten auf ägyptischen Tempelsreliefs', *VT* 25 (1975), 413–69; A. Spalinger, 'A Canaanite ritual found in Egyptian reliefs', *Journal of the Society for the Study of Egyptian Antiquities* 8 (1978), 47–60. It has been claimed that there is an allusion to human sacrifice in a Ugaritic text *KTU* 1.119.31 (= *RS* 24.266, obverse, l. 14), cf. A. Herdner, 'Une prière à Baal des ugaritiens en danger', *CRAIBL* (1972), 693–703, in *Ugaritica* VII (Paris, 1978), pp. 31–8; B. Margalit, '(RS 24.266) תפילה אוגרית לעת מצור', *Proceedings of the Seventh World Congress of Jewish Studies: Studies in the Bible and the Ancient Near East* 177 (1981), pp. 63–83 (Hebrew Section), and 'Why King Mesha of Moab sacrificed his oldest son', *BARev* 12, no. 6 (Nov./Dec., 1986), 62–3, 76. They render 'A first-born, Baal, we shall sacrifice', but the crucial word []*kr* restored to [*b*]*kr* 'first-born' could equally be [*d*]*kr* 'male'. Cf. P. Xella, 'Un testo ugaritico recente (RS 24.266, verso. 9–19 e il "sacrificio dei primi nati"', *RSF* 6 (1978), 127–36. For a general study of human sacrifice throughout the ancient near east, cf. A. R. W. Green, *The Role of Human Sacrifice in the Ancient Near East* (*ASOR* Dissertation Series 1, Missoula, 1975).

12 T. H. Gaster, *Myth, Legend and Custom in the Old Testament* (London, 1969), pp. 586–7; Weinfeld, 'The worship of Molech', p. 141.

13 *Ibid.*, pp. 140–1.

further alleges in support of his position – and this appears to be his fundamental argument – that there are significant differences between the terminology used of the Molech cult in Leviticus and that used in the prophets, Psalms, Deuteronomy and Deuteronomistic history. The former, being legal material, uses precise language and makes no allusion to slaying, sacrificing or burning in the fire (*šḥṭ*, *zbḥ*, *śrp b'š*), terms found elsewhere and held to be polemical, but rather speaks of giving to make to pass (*ntn lh'byr*) or simply giving (*ntn*). Against this, however, it may be doubted for a start whether it is correct to divide the material this way into polemical and non-polemical passages. Surely Leviticus, with its reference to playing the harlot after Molech (Lev. 20.5) and its many allusions to the abominations of the Canaanites, is just as polemical as the other parts of the Old Testament. On the other hand, this does not mean that Weinfeld's so-called polemical allusions are any the less accurate for that in their allusions to human sacrifice, which, as we have seen, is well attested in the Canaanite world in independent classical sources as well as Punic texts and archaeological evidence.[14] The expression *h'byr* is common to both Weinfeld's groups of material, as is *ntn* (cf. *ntn* in Lev. 20.2, 4; Ezek. 16.36; *h'byr* in Lev. 18.21; Jer. 32.35; Ezek. 20.31, etc.). Clearly the meaning of *h'byr* is the crucial point. We have already seen that the allusions in Ezek. 16.21 and 23.37 are explicitly glossed so as to make the sacrificial interpretation, but Weinfeld will tell us that this is polemical. What clearly cannot be described as polemical is the use of *h'byr* in connection with the offering of the first-born to Yahweh in Ezek. 20.26 and Exod. 13.12f. In the former passage Yahweh declares: 'and I defiled them through their very gifts in making them offer (*b^{e}ha'^{a}ḇīr*) all their first-born, that I might horrify them; I did it that they might know that I am the Lord.' The fact that the verb 'horrify' (*'^{a}šimmēm*) is used in connection with the offering of the first-born makes sense only on the sacrificial interpretation. Similarly, in the second passage (Exod. 13.12f) we read: 'you shall set apart (*w^{e}ha'^{a}ḇartā*) to the Lord all that first opens the womb. All the firstlings of your cattle that are males shall be the Lord's. Every firstling of an ass you shall redeem with a lamb, or if you will not redeem it you shall break its neck. Every first-born of man among your sons you shall redeem.' Now what is meant by 'you shall set apart' (*w^{e}ha'^{a}ḇartā*) is clearly indicated three verses later in Exod. 13.15, where the explanation is given: 'For when Pharaoh stubbornly refused to let us go, the Lord slew all the first-born in the land of

14 Cf. above, p. 18, n. 11.

Egypt, both the first-born of man and the first-born of cattle. Therefore I *sacrifice* (*zōḇēaḥ*) to the Lord all the males that first open the womb; but all the first-born of my sons I redeem.' This makes it clear that *h'byr* really does mean 'sacrifice', since no one can claim that this is a 'polemical' passage. The implications of Exod. 13.15 are overlooked by Weinfeld and Carroll in their discussions of Exod. 13 in connection with the Molech cult.[15]

It is clear from the Old Testament, therefore, that *h'byr* is a sacrificial term and not a term used simply to denote dedication. In no case is the latter meaning attested. The root cause of the belief that something less than sacrifice is intended would seem to be the curious expression 'pass through the fire', which has traditionally been employed to translate the Hebrew *h'byr b'š* used in connection with the Molech cult. It is true that in Num. 31.23, in a quite different context, *h'byr b* means 'pass through': Num. 31.22f states, 'only the gold, the silver, the bronze, the iron, the tin, and the lead, everything that can stand the fire, you shall pass through the fire (*ta'ᵃḇīrū ḇā'ēš*), and it shall be clean. Nevertheless it shall also be purified with the water of impurity; and whatever cannot stand the fire, you shall pass through the water (*ta'ᵃḇīrū ḇammāyim*).' So far as *h'byr b'š* means 'pass through the fire', Num. 31.23 indicates that it implies actual burning when it is a question of combustible substances, and Morton Smith has used this as an argument against Weinfeld.[16] In view of the evidence for the sacrificial nature of the Molech cult, however, it may be suggested that *h'byr b'š lmlk* means rather 'offer up/devote/pass over in the fire to Molech'; in other words, we should understand the victim as being passed into the fire, not through the fire. This meaning of *h'byr b'š* has long had supporters, e.g. in the nineteenth century in Gesenius and Kuenen.[17]

Rabbinical views on the nature of the Molech cult

At this point it may be noted that Snaith[18] and Weinfeld[19] appeal to rabbinic evidence in support of their view that the Molech cult

15 Cf. Weinfeld, 'The worship of Molech', p. 141; Carroll, *From Chaos to Covenant*, pp. 303f.

16 Morton Smith, 'A note on burning babies', *JAOS* 95 (1975), 478. Cf. Weinfeld's reply, 'Burning babies in ancient Israel. A rejoinder to Morton Smith's article in *JAOS* 95 (1975), pp. 477–479', *UF* 10 (1978), 411–13.

17 W. Gesenius, *Thesaurus philologicus criticus linguae Hebraeae et Chaldaeae Veteris Testamenti* (Leipzig, 1829–58), p. 985; A. Kuenen, 'Critische bijdragen tot de geschiedenis van den Israëlietischen godsdienst I. De integriteit van Ex. XIII: 11–16', *Theologisch Tijdschrift* 1 (1867), 63.

18 'The cult of Molech', pp. 123–4. 19 'The worship of Molech', pp. 142–4.

involved cultic dedication rather than human sacrifice. The rabbis, in fact, attest three major interpretations of the Molech cult.[20] The first interpretation understood giving up one's child to Molech as an allusion to consecrating one's child to idolatrous worship. As well as in specific rabbinic sources and some Targums, this understanding is found in the Samaritan tradition (both Hebrew and Aramaic), the LXX and other Greek versions, and the Vulgate. In the second century, the Tannaitic Rabbi Judah ben Elai understood the ritual of passing through the fire as one of covenantal initiation (Sifre on Deut. 18.10). The early fourth-century Rab Abaye described the rite as involving walking along a pile of bricks with fire on either side of it, whilst his contemporary Rabah said that it was like children leaping about on Purim (Babylonian Talmud, *Sanhedrin* 64b), which presumably alludes to a game played at Purim in which children jumped over a fire in a pit. The medieval Jewish commentator Rashi tells us that the Molech cult involved a father's giving up his son to pagan priests who caused the child to pass between two flaming pyres. As Vermes says,[21] this rabbinic reinterpretation of the prohibition of human sacrifice to Molech in terms of idolatrous worship generally served to make the biblical law 'meaningful in an age when the smoke of human sacrifice was no longer seen in the Hinnom valley'.

There was, however, a second rabbinic interpretation of the biblical prohibition about Molech. This understood it as forbidding sexual relations with a pagan woman, the idea being that the children would thereby be saved from idolatry. An early attestation of this interpretation is found in the Mishnah, *Megillah* 4.9, where we read: 'He who renders *ūmizzarʿᵃḵā lōʾ ṯittēn lᵉhaʿᵃḇīr lammōleḵ* as, "And you shall not give of your seed to cause pregnancy in a gentile woman",[22] they shall silence him with a sharp rebuke.' Though condemned in the Mishnah, this interpretation is found in the Neofiti and Pseudo-Jonathan Targums and also, it should be noted, in the Syriac Peshiṭta, even though the latter shows no direct verbal dependence on the Targums in this passage. It is clear from Tannaitic tradition transmitted in the name of Rabbi Ishmael ben Elisha and

20 For this section I am especially indebted to G. Vermes, 'Leviticus 18:21 in ancient Jewish Bible exegesis' in J. J. Petuchowski and E. Fleischer (eds.), *Studies in Aggadah, Targum and Jewish Liturgy in Memory of Joseph Heinemann* (Jerusalem, 1981), pp. 108–24. 21 *Ibid.*, p. 112.

22 'Gentile woman' is literally 'Aramean' in the text of the Mishnah here. This follows the better rendering preserved by the Cambridge manuscript Add. 470 II, Parma 138, and the Kaufmann codex from Budapest, which have *ʾrmy(y)tʾ/h* instead of *ʾrmywtʾ* 'Aramaism', which is given in most printed editions of Megillah. Cf. L. Tetzner, *Die Mischna Megilla* (Berlin, 1968), p. 143.

his school that this interpretation was concerned to stop the spread of idolatry through mixed marriages, so that we should not regard it as a ban on proselyte marriages. As we have seen, this exegesis is condemned in the Mishnah: Vermes[23] believes that the reason for its fall from favour is to be sought in the anti-Zealot attitudes of the last Tannaitic generation, which attempted to improve relations with the authorities by removing vestiges of Zealotism.

There was, finally, a third rabbinic interpretation of the Molech prohibition which needs to be noted. This is found in the Mishnah, *Sanhedrin* 7.4 and became *halakah.* Here we read: 'He who gives any of his seed to Molech is guilty only if he gives (the child) to Molech, and causes it to pass through the fire. If he gave it to Molech but did not cause it to pass through the fire, or if he caused it to pass through the fire but did not give it to Molech, he is not guilty. He must both give it to Molech and cause it to pass through the fire.' As Vermes says,[24] this ruling made the law prohibiting the Molech cult completely redundant. It thereby had the effect of invalidating exegesis number two.

All these rabbinic reinterpretations of the biblical prohibition of Molech worship are of historical interest. However, in the light of what has been said earlier, it is clear that they do not reflect the original meaning of the biblical text, and therefore, *contra* Snaith and Weinfeld, cannot be used as evidence to support their view that the Molech cult involved cultic dedication rather than human sacrifice. It is of interest to note that the rabbinic ignorance of the true nature of the Molech cult is comparable with the rabbis' ignorance of another aspect of syncretistic worship, namely the true nature of the Asherim, which they wrongly regarded as living trees rather than poles sacred to the goddess Asherah.

Leviticus 18.21

It is clear that the sexual interpretation of the Molech cult found in some rabbinic sources and still represented in a few modern scholars takes its origin from Lev. 18.21, for here the command, 'You shall not give any of your children to devote them to Molech, and so profane the name of your God: I am the Lord', comes towards the end of a section of the Holiness Code condemning various illicit sexual relationships (Lev. 18.6–23). One can understand how it might be felt

23 Cf. 'Leviticus 18:21', p. 122. 24 *Ibid.*, p. 118.

surprising that a cult thought to involve human sacrifice should be cited in a list of adulterous and other sexually deviant relationships. One modern attempt to deal with this problem is that of K. Elliger,[25] who has been followed by W. Zimmerli:[26] this view supposes that it was the children of sacred prostitutes who were offered up to Molech. However, there is no evidence to support this speculation.

The clue to what must surely be the correct explanation of the sexual context of the Molech allusion in Lev. 18.21 lies in the one other passage dealing with Molech in the Holiness Code (Lev. 20.2–5), specifically Lev. 20.5, though curiously its relevance has not hitherto been noted. There engaging in the Molech cult is referred to as 'playing the harlot after Molech', a vivid sexual metaphor which may be compared with another passage in the Holiness Code, Lev. 17.7, where offering sacrifices to satyrs is similarly spoken of as playing the harlot after them. Interestingly, this imagery is employed of human sacrifice in two other places, surely including the Molech cult, i.e. Ezek. 23.37, 'For they have committed adultery, and blood is upon their hands; with their idols they have committed adultery; and they have even offered up to them for food the sons whom they had borne to me', and Ps. 106.37–9, 'They sacrificed their sons and their daughters to the demons; they poured out innocent blood, the blood of their sons and daughters, whom they sacrificed to the idols of Canaan; and the land was polluted with blood. Thus they became unclean by their acts, and played the harlot in their doings'.

However, the important thing for our purpose is that the parallel Molech passage to Lev. 18.21 in Lev. 20.5 suggests that the former reference is set in a sexual context because the Molech cult is thought of metaphorically as an adulterous one *vis-à-vis* Yahweh. The ease with which the Old Testament slips from speaking of literal adultery to spiritual adultery is well known (cf. Jer. 3.1, 2, 6, 8–9). Indeed, it is significant that we find this very thing in Lev. 20. The theme common to the laws in that chapter from verses 1–21 is that of adultery, but whereas the first two refer to playing the harlot after Molech and ghosts and spirits respectively (vv. 5, 6), the remaining laws are concerned with literally adulterous or otherwise sexually deviant relationships (vv. 10–21). The latter laws are indeed remarkably similar to those in Lev. 18, the context into which the commandment

25 'Das Gesetz Leviticus 18', *ZAW* 67 (1955), 17, reprinted in his book *Kleine Schriften zum Alten Testament* (Munich, 1966), p. 250.

26 *Ezechiel*, vol. 1 (Neukirchen-Vluyn, 1969), p. 357 (ET, *Ezekiel*, vol. 1 [Philadelphia, 1979], p. 344).

about Molech is set. There is, therefore, every reason to believe that the law about Molech in Lev. 18.21 is set in its present context because the cult is thought of as involving a spiritually adulterous relationship, just as in Lev. 20.5. The only difference is that in Lev. 18.21 the law is set more *in mediis rebus*, so to speak. However, with regard to this, it should be remembered that the Old Testament was capable of slipping very easily from the thought of literal to spiritual adultery, as was noted above, and that whereas the laws before the verse are concerned with literal adultery (vv. 6–20), those which follow refer to other sexual deviations (vv. 22–3), namely homosexuality and bestiality. We thus have the not unnatural sequence of literal adultery, spiritual adultery, and then other sexual deviations. Finally, as other scholars have noted,[27] the precise positioning of the Molech passage is conditioned by the use of the *Stichwörter lō ᵓtittēn* and *zeraᶜ* which it shares with the immediately preceding verse.

Topheth

The place where the human sacrifices to Molech took place in the Hinnom valley is referred to as Topheth (*tōpeṯ*), and is mentioned in 2 Kgs. 23.10; Jer. 7.31, 32, 19.6, 11, 12, 13, 14, and it also occurs in the form *topteh* in Isa. 30.33 as part of the imagery employed to depict the coming destruction of the Assyrians. What are the etymology and meaning of this word? Nowadays it is generally connected with Aramaic *taṗyā*, Syriac *tᵉpayā* or *tᵉpāyā* and Arabic *ᵓuṯfīyā*, and the conclusion is sometimes drawn that it is an Aramaic loan word. This is something I shall discuss presently. First of all, however, I shall note earlier suggestions in the history of scholarship on this question.[28] The first two points express rabbinic views:

(i) Topheth was connected with Hebrew *pth* 'to entice', cf. the Babylonian Talmud, *ᶜErubin* 19a.

(ii) It was connected with Hebrew *tpp* 'to sound the timbrel'. Cf. Abarbanel in his commentary on Lev. 20.1ff: 'The children, as they expired, cried out loudly owing to the intensity of the fire. In order not to arouse the compassion of father and mother at the wailing and crying of their sons, the pagan priests sounded the "topheth", to

27 B. Baentsch, *Exodus-Leviticus-Numeri* (Göttingen, 1903), p. 394; Elliger, 'Das Gesetz Leviticus 18', p. 15, reprinted in his *Kleine Schriften*, p. 247.

28 Some earlier suggestions are listed in the article by S. D. F. Salmond on 'Tophet, Topheth' in J. Hastings (ed.), *A Dictionary of the Bible*, vol. 4 (Edinburgh, 1902), p. 799.

confuse the listeners and prevent the screams of the children from being heard.' Compare also Rashi on Jer. 7.31 and Ḳimḥi on 2 Kgs. 23.10.

The view that Topheth is to be connected with *tpp* 'to sound the timbrel' was also held in more recent times, e.g. by H. Bonar,[29] who, noting the allusion to *tuppīm* 'timbrels' in Isa. 30.32, shortly before the reference to Topheth in Isa. 30.33, understood Topheth to mean 'music-grove'.

(iii) Jerome (in his commentary on Jer. 7.31) interpreted Topheth as meaning *latitudo*, probably deriving it from *pth*.

(iv) Others have connected the word Topheth with Persian *tōften* 'to burn'.[30]

(v) Topheth has also been connected with the Egyptian name *Θωύθ* or *Θώθ*.[31]

(vi) In the light of Jerome's description of the place, it has been thought that its name alluded to its beauty. Thus, E. F. C. Rosenmüller[32] connected it with Hebrew *yph* 'to be fair'.

(vii) Perhaps not surprisingly, in view of the existence of the word *tōpeṯ* meaning '(act of) spitting', from the root *tūp̱*, which occurs in Job 17.6, it was suggested that the Topheth mentioned in connection with the Molech cult meant, by an understandable semantic development, 'place of abhorrence/abomination'.[33] Interestingly, whilst this view is no longer followed, H. Haag,[34] in his *Bibel-Lexikon*, nevertheless thinks it possible that the *vowels* of the Molech Topheth are a deliberate word-play on the other word Topheth. More usually in recent times it has been thought to be the vowels of *bōšeṯ* 'shame' which have been inserted in the word, just as in Molech.[35] (If so, the LXX's vocalization *Ταφεθ* may indicate the original pronunciation.)

(viii) Some have connected Topheth with Hebrew *tūp̱īnē* 'baked

29 'Topheth' in W. Smith (ed.), *A Dictionary of the Bible* (London, 1863), vol. 3, p. 1563.

30 E.g. J. Simonis, *Onomasticum Veteris Testamenti* (Halle, 1741), p. 124; Gesenius, *Thesaurus philologicus*, p. 1497. Others, e.g. F. Boettcher, *De inferis*, vol. 1 (Dresden, 1845), §168, p. 80, and §176, p. 85, saw this as the origin of the word Topheth but thought that on being taken up into Hebrew its form was conformed to the word *tōpeṯ* 'spitting, abomination'. Cf. below no. (vii).

31 Cf. A. Müller, *Glossarium Sacrum* (Frankfurt, 1690), pp. 102f.

32 *Scholia in Vetus Testamentum. Partis octavae, Ieremiae vaticinia et Threnos continentis, volumen primum* (Leipzig, 1826), p. 269.

33 E.g. E. C. A. Riehm (ed.), *Handwörterbuch des Biblischen Altertums*, vol. 2 (Bielefeld and Leipzig, 1884), p. 1681 (*sub* Topheth). For the more nuanced view of F. Boettcher and others, see above, n. 30.

34 'Tophet' in *Bibel-Lexikon*, 2nd edn (Einsiedeln, Zurich and Cologne, 1968), col. 1766.

35 Cf. below, pp. 56–8.

pieces(?)' (Lev. 6.14, ET 21),[36] the root of which may be *ʾph* 'to bake'. As we shall see, this view is not to be dissociated from the next view, although this is not generally realized nowadays.

(ix) It was as a result of the work of W. Robertson Smith[37] that the view which is now generally followed[38] gained acceptance. He connected the word Topheth with Aramaic *tap̱yā* 'stove, fireplace, pot', Syriac *t*^{e}*payā* (or *t*^{e}*p̱āyā*) 'bake-house, oven, kettle, three-legged caldron', and Arabic *ʾuṯfīyā* 'the stone (which is one of three) whereon the cooking-pot is placed', the last-mentioned being a loan-word from the Aramaic.[39] Smith saw Hebrew Topheth as a loan-word from the Aramaic. This fitted in with his view on the Aramaic origin of the Molech cult, and he compared the Aramean influence on Ahaz in the matter of the altar in 2 Kgs. 16. What further seemed to support the view that Topheth was an Aramaic loan-word was that it appeared to be cognate with the Hebrew root *špt* 'to set (on the fire)' – used of a pot in 2 Kgs. 4.38 and Ezek. 24.3. Since according to the rule of Semitic phonetics, where Aramaic has *t* in common with proto-Semitic, Hebrew should have *š*, the fact that Hebrew has *t*, unlike the case with *špt*, suggested that the word Topheth was directly borrowed from the Aramaic. This in turn might suggest that the Molech cult was of Aramean origin, since this cult and Topheth seem to be constantly associated.

What are we to say of all this? An Aramean origin for the Molech cult seems unlikely, since all the Old Testament evidence strongly suggests that it is Canaanite.[40] On the other hand, this does not mean that the etymological connection with the Aramaic word *tap̱yā* is to be rejected, as H. Wildberger hints.[41] The meaning 'fire-place' fits it admirably – compare the context in Isa. 30.33: 'For Topheth has long been prepared; yea, for the king it is made ready, its pyre made deep and wide,[42] with fire and wood in abundance; the breath of the Lord, like a stream of brimstone, kindles it.' However, it would seem that ever since Robertson Smith, scholars have been wrong in assuming

36 S. Bochart, *Phaleg et Canaan* (Leiden, 1707), col. 528, who also connects *tōpeṯ* with Greek τύφειν 'to burn'.

37 *Lectures on the Religion of the Semites*, 2nd edn (London, 1894), p. 377, n. 2.

38 E.g., cf. *KB*, under *tōpeṯ*; J. Gray, *I & II Kings*, 3rd edn (London, 1977), pp. 735f.

39 Cf. S. Fraenkel, *Die aramäischen Fremdwörter im Arabischen* (Leiden, 1886), p. 63.

40 Cf. below, pp. 29–31.

41 *Jesaja*, vol. 3 (Neukirchen-Vluyn, 1982), p. 1223.

42 Cf. above, p. 17, n. 7.

that Topheth is cognate with Hebrew *špt* and therefore an Aramaic loan-word. According to R. Payne Smith's *Thesaurus Syriacus*,[43] *tᵉp̱ayā* (or *tᵉp̱āyā*) derives from the verbal root *ʾpʾ* 'to bake', and this seems admirably suitable. If this is the case, Topheth cannot also be cognate with Hebrew *špt*, and further examination of the latter root confirms this conclusion. It is true that in both 2 Kgs. 4.38 and Ezek. 24.3 the meaning 'to set' which it bears is used specifically of setting a pot on a fire. However, it is clear that the verb has no special fiery associations and is used of setting generally. Thus, in Ps. 22.16 (ET 15), it is used of ordaining peace: 'O Lord, thou wilt ordain (*tišpōṯ*) peace for us.' It is also relevant to note that Ugaritic *ṯpd* 'to set, put' (used of El's setting his foot on the footstool) may well be cognate with Hebrew *špt*, thus further illustrating the general background of setting to which *špt* alludes and lack of specific reference to setting on a fire.

At this point it should also be noted that Robertson Smith and others subsequently have further sought to connect Topheth with the root *špt* by appealing to the Hebrew word *ʾašpōṯ*, allegedly meaning 'ash-heap'. Thus Smith writes, 'In nomad life the fireplace of one day is the ash-heap of the next',[44] and *BDB* gives the meaning of *ʾašpōṯ* as 'ash-heap (?), refuse-heap, dung-hill', and explains that its original meaning was probably 'fire-place stones', appealing to the Arabic *ʾuṯfīyā*, the same word as is generally associated with Topheth. However, against this it should be noted that the evidence of all the ancient Versions as well as rabbinic Hebrew unanimously supports the meaning 'dung' or 'dunghill' for *ʾašpōṯ* and lends no support to the rendering 'ash-heap'. Accordingly, it is too remote semantically to be likely to belong to the same root as Topheth 'fire-place, oven' and there is every reason to believe that the latter is from the stem *ʾph* 'to bake'. The word *tup̱īnē* in Lev. 6.14 (ET 21), if it means 'baked pieces', as is widely believed, would also be a similar formation from the root *ʾph*, and like Topheth also lacks the aleph.

The conclusion of this discussion is that, though Hebrew Topheth is cognate with Aramaic *tap̱yā*, Syriac *tᵉp̱ayā* or *tᵉp̱āyā* and also Arabic *ʾuṯfīyā*,[45] there are no grounds for supposing it to be an

43 Vol. 1 (Oxford, 1879), col. 328.

44 *Religion of the Semites*, p. 377, n. 2.

45 W. F. Albright, *Yahweh and the Gods of Canaan* (London, 1968), p. 327, suggests that instead of being an Aramaic loan-word *tōp̱eṯ* may be a dialectical form, like Hebrew *yᵉṯannū* (for *yᵉšannū*) in Judg. 5.11. In suggesting this, Albright supposes

Aramaic loan-word. This conclusion is wholly what one would expect, since the Old Testament unanimously indicates that the associated Molech cult was Canaanite rather than Aramean in origin.

that *tōpeṯ* is cognate with Hebrew *špt* 'to place' and *ʾašpōṯ* 'dung', but we have already seen that there are no convincing grounds for maintaining this connection. Accordingly, there is no reason to suppose that the *t* in *tōpeṯ* is a dialectal variant of *š*. Albright's supposition that Hebrew *mišpᵉṯayim* (Gen. 49.14; Judg. 5.16) and *šᵉpattayim* (Ps. 68.14, ET 13) are the dual of a word meaning 'hearth, fire-place' and that Ugaritic *mṯpdm* likewise means 'two fire-places' seems dubious.

3
The background and identity of Molech and his relationship to Yahweh

The Old Testament evidence for the Canaanite origin of the Molech cult

I have established earlier that Molech was a divine name or title. He was, moreover, a deity to whom children were offered up in fiery sacrifices. What, then, was the origin of this deity and cult? The Old Testament gives every indication that its background is to be seen as Canaanite. This is the case both in places where Molech is explicitly named and also in places where the allusion is implicit. I shall note first the evidence of explicit allusions. First of all, it is significant that the Molech cult mentioned in Lev. 18.21 is one of a series of abominations which are explicitly dubbed as Canaanite. Thus, just three to four verses after the Molech reference, we read in Lev. 18.24–5: 'Do not defile yourselves by any of these things, for by all these the nations I am casting out before you defiled themselves; and the land became defiled, so that I punished its iniquity, and the land vomited out its inhabitants.' Then, a little further on, in verse 27, we read: 'for all these abominations the men of the land did, who were before you, so that the land became defiled.' Finally, it is noteworthy that the list of abominations is prefaced in verse 3 by the words: 'You shall not do as they do in the land of Egypt, where you dwelt, and shall not do as they do in the land of Canaan, to which I am bringing you. You shall not walk in their statutes.' The mention of Egypt alongside Canaan here in this one instance is without parallel and is clearly an artificial intrusion arising from the fact that in their present position the laws of Lev. 18 have their context in the legislation allegedly given by Moses following the Exodus from Egypt. It is also important to notice that the other Molech passage in Leviticus (20.2–5) forms part of a series of prohibitions leading up to the statement, 'And you shall not walk in the customs of the nation which

I am casting out before you; for they did all these things, and therefore I abhorred them' (Lev. 20.23).

Another explicit allusion to the Molech cult is in 2 Kgs. 23.10, where we read that 'Josiah defiled Topheth, which is in the valley of the sons of Hinnom, that no one might offer up his son or daughter in the fire to Molech.' The only human sacrifices in Judah referred to in the immediately preceding chapters are those of Ahaz in 2 Kgs. 16.3 and Manasseh in 2 Kgs. 21.6, who both offered up a son, and these are clearly to be seen in relation with this Molech cult. Now the contexts in which the acts of both Ahaz and Manasseh are set make it clear that they are to be seen as deriving from Canaanite custom, for 2 Kgs. 16.3 states explicitly that Ahaz 'even offered up his son in the fire, according to the abominable practices of the nations whom the Lord drove out before the people of Israel', and 2 Kgs. 21.2, in introducing the list of Manasseh's abominations which includes his offering of human sacrifice, declares that 'he did what was evil in the sight of the Lord, according to the abominable practices of the nations whom the Lord drove out before the people of Israel', and verse 11 states further that 'Manasseh king of Judah has committed these abominations, and has done things more wicked than all that the Amorites did, who were before him'.

A further reference to Molech is in Isa. 57.9[1] (cf. too the allusion to human sacrifice in verse 5), and it is significant that his cult is condemned in the same breath as the syncretistic Canaanite fertility cult associated with the high places, in verses 5, 7, and 9, thereby suggesting a similar Canaanite background for Molech. Again, Jer. 32.35 indicates a close connection between Molech and the Canaanite Baal when it declares that 'They built the high places of Baal in the valley of the son of Hinnom to offer up their sons and daughters to Molech', with which one may compare Jer. 19.5, where, in referring to the same cult, the deity is simply called Baal.

It is probable that the Molech cult is included in the condemnation in Ezek. 16.20–1, 36, where reference is again made to human sacrifice in this same general period. Once more, therefore, it is significant that the context indicates a Canaanite background. This is explicitly stated in Ezek. 16.2–3, where Yahweh declares: 'Son of man, make known to Jerusalem her abominations, and say, Thus says the Lord God to Jerusalem: Your origin and your birth are of the land of the Canaanites; your father was an Amorite, and your mother

1 Cf. below, pp. 50–2.

a Hittite.' Compare again, verse 45: 'Your mother was a Hittite and your father an Amorite.' Another passage alluding to the Canaanite background of human sacrifice in Israel, doubtless including the Molech cult, is Ps. 106.37–8: 'They sacrificed their sons and their daughters to the demons; they poured out innocent blood, the blood of their sons and daughters, whom they sacrificed to the idols of Canaan; and the land was polluted with their blood.'

That the temptation to participate in rites of human sacrifice came from the Canaanites is further indicated by Deut. 12.31 and 18.9–10. The former passage states, 'for every abominable thing which the Lord hates they [*sc.* the Canaanites] have done for their gods; for they even burn their sons and their daughters in the fire to their gods', whilst the latter declares, 'When you come into the land which the Lord your God gives you, you shall not learn to follow the abominable practices of those nations [*sc.* of Canaan]. There shall not be found among you any one who offers up his son or daughter in the fire.' It is likely that the Molech cult is included in the condemnations in these verses (cf. the references in the Deuteronomist cited earlier), even though it may not be exclusively in mind.

In the light of all these texts, it may be claimed that the Old Testament, in its various writings, unanimously supports the view that the Molech cult was taken over from the Canaanites. Other peoples certainly practised human sacrifice[2] – compare the fact that Mesha king of Moab offered up his eldest son, according to 2 Kgs. 3.27 – but the Old Testament makes it abundantly clear that the Molech cult was appropriated specifically from the Canaanites.

Who was Molech?

It has already been shown that Molech in the Old Testament is to be understood as a divine name. But who exactly was Molech? Various views have been put forward and these must now be considered in turn.

Milcom

The first view that I am going to consider is that Molech is the same deity as Milcom, the god of the Ammonites. It is perhaps not

2 Cf. A. R. W. Green, *The Role of Human Sacrifice in the Ancient Near East* (*ASOR* Dissertation Series 1, Missoula, 1975).

surprising that a number of scholars have adopted this view,[3] since the names are very similar, the only difference in the unvocalized Hebrew text being the addition of the letter *mem* at the end of the form Milcom. Moreover, 1 Kgs. 11.7 actually refers to 'Molech the abomination of the Ammonites' as one of the deities to whom Solomon erected a high place on the mountain east of Jerusalem. However, there can be no doubt that the reading Molech is here a slip for Milcom,[4] as the parallel references to 'Milcom the abomination of the Ammonites' in 1 Kgs. 11.5, 33 show (cf. 2 Kgs. 23.13). The Lucianic recension of the LXX actually reads *Μελχομ* and the Peshiṭta reads *malkōm* (i.e. Milcom) in 1 Kgs. 11.7.

Moreover, there are good grounds for believing that Molech is not simply to be equated with Milcom. First, it should be pointed out that the Old Testament clearly distinguishes the two deities: it speaks of Milcom when referring to the national god of the Ammonites and Molech when alluding to rites of human sacrifice. Moreover, 2 Kgs. 23.10, 13 mention both deities within the space of a few verses and clearly distinguish them, since verse 10 refers to Molech with his rites of human sacrifice as having his cult centre in the Hinnom valley, whereas verse 13 speaks of Milcom, the abomination of the Ammonites, as having his cult centre to the south of the mount of corruption, east of Jerusalem. A second argument against the simple equation of Molech and Milcom is the fact that the Old Testament consistently indicates that the former was appropriated from the Canaanites whereas the latter is god of the Ammonites.

However, although Molech is not simply to be equated with Milcom, in the present state of our knowledge the possibility cannot be ruled out that there was ultimately an underlying connection between the two deities. In spite of the discovery in recent years of Ammonite inscriptions referring to Milcom,[5] our knowledge of this deity is still too scanty to form a positive judgment on this question. It is interesting to note, however, as we shall see later,[6] that in the Ugaritic texts there was a god *mlk*, doubtless the prototype of

3 E.g. G. C. O'Ceallaigh, 'And *so* David did to *all the cities* of Ammon', *VT* 12 (1962), 185–9. 4 Cf. below, p. 74.

5 According to K. P. Jackson, *The Ammonite Language of the Iron Age* (Chico, 1983), p. 98, the name Milcom occurs on an Ammonite seal (cf. p. 74) and in the first word of the Amman citadel inscription (cf. p. 10), if this is correctly restored as [*m*]*lkm*. According to G. C. Heider, *The Cult of Molek: A Reassessment* (Sheffield, 1985), p. 170, the name Milcom occurs on two further Ammonite seals, but he cites L. G. Herr, *The Scripts of Ancient Northwest Semitic Seals* (Missoula, 1978), pp. 74f, who holds that these two seals are probably forgeries.

6 Cf. below, pp. 46f.

Molech, who was associated with the place Ashtaroth in Transjordan. This location may suggest an ultimate connection between Molech and the Ammonite Milcom. However, what is clear is that, so far as the Old Testament is concerned, they were distinct gods, and Molech was appropriated from the Canaanites, not the Ammonites.

Shaḥar and Shalem-Athtar-Kemosh-Milcom

We must now consider the views of J. Gray[7] and F. Stolz,[8] which, although not identical, nevertheless have many similarities. In common with the view just discussed, Gray holds that Molech is the same deity as Milcom, noting 1 Kgs. 11.7 (wrongly cited by him as v. 8), where in the MT Molech is referred to as the abomination of the Ammonites. However, Gray's view is much more complicated than the previous one, since he does not believe that the Molech cult was originally appropriated from the Ammonites but from the Canaanites, and he posits the following series of equations: Shaḥar and Shalem = Athtar = Kemosh = Milcom = Molech. The alleged evidence for the equation of Molech and Milcom has previously been noted and its dubiety has already been pointed out, even though there may ultimately have been some connection. The other links in the chain are also too speculative to carry conviction. Thus, the evidence for the equation of Milcom and Kemosh is based on the single allusion in Judg. 11.24, where Jephthah refers to Kemosh as 'your god' in what is allegedly a message delivered to the Ammonite king.[9] However, this argument is unconvincing, since, as a matter of fact, the whole of the address in Judg. 11.15–28 is actually concerned with Moab rather than Ammon, apart from one reference to 'the land of the Ammonites' in verse 15. Thus, for example, verses 17–18 are concerned with Israel's earlier relations with Moab, verse 25 contrasts the attitude of the present king with that of Balak king of

7 'The desert god 'Aṯtr in the literature and religion of Canaan', *JNES* 8 (1949), 72–83. Cf. his book *The Legacy of Canaan,* 2nd edn (*SVT* 5, 1965), pp. 171–3.

8 *Strukturen und Figuren im Kult von Jerusalem* (*BZAW* 118, 1970), pp. 181–218.

9 Although Gray does not mention this, it should perhaps be noted, however, that in an Assyrian god list (*CT* pt. 24, 36.66) Kammus (i.e. Kemosh) is referred to as a manifestation of Nergal, the underworld god, just as Malik is equated with Nergal in O. Schroeder, *Keilschrifttexte aus Assur verschiedenen Inhalts* (Leipzig, 1920), 63.II.37. This might indicate a connection between Molech (Malik) and Kemosh. Cf. P. Jensen, 'Alttestamentlich-Keilschriftliches. II. Die Götter כְּמוֹשׁ und מֶלֶךְ und die Erscheinungsformen *Kammuš* und *Malik* des assyrisch-babylonischen Gottes *Nergal*', *Zeitschrift für Assyriologie* 42, NS 8 (1934), 235–7, where the *CT* volume is wrongly cited as being 25.

Moab, and the cities mentioned in verse 26 are known from the Old Testament and the Moabite stone to have been Moabite. Compare too Num. 21.27–30, where Sihon's kingdom (Judg. 11.19ff) was previously Moabite. The reference to the Moabite god Kemosh in verse 24 is of a piece with this and not evidence of his worship by the Ammonites.[10]

Again, with regard to the equation of Kemosh and Athtar, one needs more than the isolated allusion to Athtar-Kemosh on the Moabite Stone, line 17, to be convinced of their identity.[11] After all, we know of various compound deities where there can be no question of a basic identity between the two elements. Moreover, there is no evidence that Athtar was an underworld deity, which he should be if he is the same as Molech. Finally, with regard to the alleged equation of Shaḥar and Shalem with Athtar, it should be noted that there is no evidence of this from Ugarit: if they were identical, it is surprising that their names never occur together in poetic parallelism. It thus appears that the links in Gray's chain are weak and he has not made out his case that Molech was identical with this series of other gods.

Stolz's view is a more modest version of that of Gray, in that he simply equates Molech with Athtar and Shalem, the latter being understood as a Jebusite god of Jerusalem. However, although it is possible that Molech was appropriated from the Jebusites,[12] the objections to Molech's equation with Athtar and of Athtar's with Shalem have already been noted.

Baal

I shall next consider the view that Molech is simply another name for Baal. That certain scholars should hold this view today[13] is hardly surprising, since the Old Testament itself seems to lend some support to it. Thus, whereas Jer. 32.35 declares, 'They built the high places of Baal in the valley of the son of Hinnom, to offer up their sons and

10 For the critical questions involved here, see the discussions in the commentaries, e.g. G. F. Moore, *A Critical and Exegetical Commentary on Judges* (Edinburgh, 1895), pp. 283, 291–5; C. F. Burney, *The Book of Judges* (London, 1920), pp. 298–317; R. G. Boling, *Judges* (Garden City, 1975), pp. 201–5; J. A. Soggin, *Judges* (ET, London, 1981), pp. 209–13.

11 Cf. *KAI* 181.17.

12 Cf. below, pp. 54f.

13 Cf. L. Sabottka, *Zephanja. Versuch einer Neuübersetzung mit philologischem Kommentar* (Rome, 1972), pp. 24–5, with regard to Zeph. 1.5. Sabottka also thinks that *meleḵ* is a title of Baal in Zeph. 1.8 and perhaps also in Zeph. 3.15. See also his discussion of Zeph. 1.8 on pp. 36–8. W. Thiel, *Die deuteronomistische Redaktion von Jeremia 1–25* (*WMANT* 41, Neukirchen-Vluyn, 1973), p. 129, speaks of Molech sacrifices as an expression of the Baalized Yahweh cult. Cf. G.

daughters to Molech', a verse indicating the close relationship rather than identity of Molech and Baal, the parallel passage in Jer. 19.5 states that they 'have built the high places of Baal to burn their sons in the fire as burnt offerings to Baal', suggesting that Molech and Baal are to be equated. However, it should be noted that the crucial words 'as burnt offerings to Baal' (*ʿōlōṯ labbāʿal*) are missing from the LXX and are doubtless to be regarded as an expansion of the original Hebrew text.[14] However, two other passages in Jeremiah also deserve to be noted. The first is in Jer. 2.23, where the prophet declares: 'How can you say, "I am not defiled, I have not gone after the Baals"? Look at your way in the valley.' It is generally accepted that this must be an allusion to the Molech cult in the valley of Hinnom, in view of the reference here to 'the valley'.[15] This is probably correct. However, one cannot base too much on this verse, since (a) the prophet speaks

Östborn, *Yahweh and Baal: Studies in the Book of Hosea and Related Documents* (Lund, 1956), pp. 23, 24, 38, 42, 55–7, 81, 103, who follows H. S. Nyberg in finding a number of references to a god Melek in the book of Hosea, and regards this as a title of Baal. For a rejection of the view that Hosea refers to a god Melek, see below, pp. 75–7.

14 Cf. J. G. Janzen, *Studies in the Text of Jeremiah* (Cambridge, Mass., 1973); E. Tov, 'L'incidence de la critique textuelle sur la critique littéraire dans le livre de Jérémie', *RB* 79 (1972), 189–99.

15 J. A. Soggin, however, in '"La tua condotta nella valle", nota a Geremia 2, 23a', *RSO* 36 (1961), 207–11 (ET, '"Your conduct in the valley". A note on Jeremiah 2, 23a', *Old Testament and Oriental Studies* [Rome, 1975], pp. 78–83), maintains that the reference is to a funerary cult (cf. LXX *πολυάνδριον* 'cemetery' for Hebrew *gayʾ* 'valley'), though he does not exclude the possibility that human sacrifice may have been associated with it. However, there seems to be no real evidence for this view. Soggin follows Albright's discredited view that the high places (*bāmōṯ*), of which there was one in the Hinnom valley, were associated with the cult of the dead, and also the view that the *šᵉḏēmōṯ* of the Kidron valley (cf. 2 Kgs. 23.4; Jer. 31.40) imply a Mot cult. But the Kidron is not the same as the Hinnom valley, and as we shall see below (pp. 40–1), *šᵉḏēmōṯ* does not mean 'field of Mot'. There is no more reason to follow the LXX's rendering 'cemetery' in Jer. 2.23 than there is in Jer. 19.2, 6, where the setting is explicitly the human sacrificial cult in the Hinnom valley (cf. v. 5). Although certainty is not possible, the references to the Molech cult in the Hinnom valley elsewhere in Jeremiah and other books of the Old Testament make it probable that we have here an allusion to this cult.

W. McKane, 'Jeremiah II 23–25: observations on the versions and history of exegesis', *OTS* 17 (1972), 82, believes that the reference is not to any specific valley and he maintains that the sexual imagery in Jer. 2.24–5 does not cohere very well with human sacrifice in the Hinnom valley. However, he overlooks the fact that sexual imagery is applied to the Molech cult several times in the Old Testament (cf. Lev. 18.21 context, 20.5; Ezek. 16.20–1, 23.37). McKane believes that the reference in Jer. 2.23 is to idolatrous practices in valleys generally. However, the fact that the singular form 'valley' is employed tends to argue against this, and the prominence given to the Hinnom valley Molech cult in literature relating to this period (e.g. Jer. 7.31, 19.5, 32.35) gives a certain plausibility to the generally held view that it is the valley of Hinnom rites which are here in view.

of 'the Baals' in the plural rather than simply of Baal, and this, as is widely acknowledged, may be a way of referring to Canaanite deities in general, and (b) the verse makes it clear that the people may not have recognized that they were worshipping 'the Baals' anyway, this simply reflecting the prophet's own interpretation of their actions. The other passage worthy of note in Jeremiah is Jer. 3.24, a prose passage which reads: 'But from our youth the shameful thing has devoured all for which our fathers laboured, their flocks and their herds, their sons and their daughters.' The Hebrew expression rendered 'shameful thing' here is *bōšeṯ*, which elsewhere sometimes serves as a euphemism for the name of the god Baal (cf. Jer. 11.13; Hos. 9.10; 2 Sam. 2.8, 12, 15, etc., 4.4, 9.6–13, 11.21), and it may well be that the reference to the devouring of sons and daughters alludes to the offerings in the Molech cult. Also suggestive of a close connection between the Molech cult and Baal worship is the fact that allusions to the Molech cult, whether explicit or implicit, are so often referred to in the context of the Canaanite fertility cult, which of course, was especially centred on the god Baal (cf. Isa. 57.5–9; Ezek. 16.20–1, 24–5, 30–31).

However, whilst there was clearly a close connection between the Baalistic fertility cult and Molech, there are two decisive objections to the view that Molech and Baal are simply to be equated. First, if this were the case, it would be surprising that the deity in question is not constantly called Baal and that a distinct name Molech has to be used when he is associated with human sacrifice. The only natural conclusion to draw from this is that there was a deity distinct from Baal called Molech who was associated with human sacrifice. Secondly, and this is a related point, there are passages in the Old Testament where Baal and Molech are mentioned in close proximity as if they were separate deities. Thus, 2 Kgs. 23.5 refers *inter alia* to 'those also who burned incense to Baal', whilst only another five verses later, in verse 10, we read of Josiah's defiling of Topheth 'that no one might offer up his son or daughter in the fire to Molech'.

The clear conclusion from all this is that Molech was not Baal, but his cult was closely related to Baal's. We shall see presently, however, that in the Punic world human sacrifices were regularly offered to the god Baal-ḥammon (together with his consort Tinnit) and that, contrary to the usual understanding, this deity is to be equated with Baal, not El.[16]

16 Cf. below, pp. 37–40.

A note on Baal-ḥammon

The human sacrifices of the Carthaginians mentioned in their inscriptions are regularly represented as having been offered to the god Baal-ḥammon or to Baal-ḥammon and his consort Tinnit.[17] It seems to be widely accepted by modern scholars that Baal-ḥammon is to be equated with the god El, since the classical references to Carthaginian human sacrifice consistently refer to the recipient as Kronos,[18] and Kronos often serves to represent El, as in Philo of Byblos. The element Baal in the name Baal-ḥammon is held to be an epithet 'lord' rather than the proper name of the god Baal, so that the name signifies 'lord of ḥammon', which is customarily interpreted to mean either 'lord of the incense altar' or 'lord of Amanus'. Generally, the identification of Baal-ḥammon with El is assumed without further discussion because of the classical allusions to Kronos, but F. M. Cross[19] has sought to reinforce the case with further arguments. Understanding Baal-ḥammon to mean 'lord of Amanus', he argues that this coheres with El on the ground that Mt. Amanus was El's dwelling place. He further notes the epithet *gerontis* used of Kronos of Gadir (Cadiz), *senex* used of Saturn of New Carthage, and the epithet *saeculo* used of the African Saturn, and compares El's title *ʿōlām* 'the Ancient One'. Finally, he repeats the view of B. Landsberger[20] that the sequence of the deities in the Phoenician Kilamuwa inscription, Baal-ṣemed, Baal-ḥamman and Rakkab-El (*KAI* 24.15–16) is to be equated with the series Hadad, El and Rakkab-El in the Aramaic Hadad and Panammuwa inscriptions (*KAI* 214.2, 11, 18; 215.22). All three inscriptions, it may be noted, come from Zenjirli.

There are, however, good reasons for disputing the identity of Baal-ḥammon with El and for supposing that Baal-ḥammon is simply a manifestation of the god Baal, as the name would suggest. It is striking that the Carthaginian inscriptions never refer to the deity as El but consistently allude to him as Baal-ḥammon. This strongly suggests that Baal-ḥammon is not simply an epithet but the god's proper name. Moreover, on a number of occasions Baal-ḥammon is simply called Baal, with no accompanying epithet. That this is the case is clear from the fact that we find dedications not only of the type

17 E.g. *KAI* 103.1, 105.3, 106.1, 107.1.
18 Cf. below, pp. 86–91, for translations of the classical sources.
19 *Canaanite Myth and Hebrew Epic* (Cambridge, Mass., 1973), pp. 24ff.
20 *Samʾal* (Ankara, 1948), p. 47, n. 117.

'To the lord to Baal-ḥammon and to the lady, to Tinnit' (e.g. *KAI* 105.1), but also of the type 'To the lord to Baal and to Tinnit face of Baal' (e.g. *KAI* 137.1). Moreover, there are many dedications to Baal-ḥammon and Tinnit in which Tinnit is referred to as 'face of Baal', which can only mean Baal-ḥammon alluded to in the same context (e.g. *KAI* 85.1, 'To the lady, to Tinnit face of Baal and to the lord Baal-ḥammon'; cf. similarly *KAI* 79.1, 86.1, 94.1, 97.1). It is abundantly obvious, therefore, that Tinnit's consort can be referred to equally as Baal-ḥammon and as Baal. This strongly suggests, therefore, that for the Carthaginians Baal-ḥammon was a form of Baal rather than of El. With this coheres the fact that, in Latin inscriptions, he bears the epithets *frugifer* and *deus frugum*,[21] indicating a fertility god, which does not suit El very well although it fits Baal admirably. Further, Baal-ḥammon's consort was called Tinnit,[22] and whilst there is dispute over her precise identification – Anat or Astarte are often thought to be intended – a text from Sarepta in Phoenicia refers to the compound deity Tinnit-Astarte,[23] and, as is well known, Astarte was Baal's consort. As for the name Baal-ḥammon, it is unlikely that the second element represents the name of Mt. Amanus, since it seems unlikely that the chief Carthaginian deity should be named after such a remote north Syrian mountain, which was already distant from the original Phoenician homeland. On the other hand, the meaning 'lord of the incense altar',[24] which is most commonly accepted,[25] is readily explicable when it is noted that a number of depictions of Baal-ḥammon's cult feature an incense altar.[26] In any case, the evidence for El's being

21 E.g. *CILat* 8.2666, 4581, 8711, 8826=20628, 17677, 17720, 20710.

22 On this goddess see F. O. Hvidberg-Hansen, *La Déesse TNT* (2 vols., Copenhagen, 1979).

23 J. B. Pritchard, *Recovering Sarepta, a Phoenician City* (Princeton, 1978), pp. 105ff.

24 Cf. Hebrew *ḥammān* 'incense altar' (on which see below, n. 25). The root is surely *ḥmm* 'to be hot', in which case there is no connection with Ugaritic *ḥmn* mentioned in cultic contexts (cf. *KTU* 1.112.3, 8; 1.106.13, 14; *RIH* 77/2B.1), which may possibly refer to Mt. Amanus.

25 Cf. H. Ingholt, 'Le sens du mot Ḥammān' in *Mélanges Syriens offerts à Monsieur René Dussaud*, vol. 2 (Paris, 1939), pp. 799–801; *KAI*, vol. 2, p. 77; K. Galling, 'Baʿal Ḥammon in Kition und die ḥammanîm' in H. Gese and H. P. Rüger (eds.), *Wort und Geschichte. Festschrift für Karl Elliger zum 70. Geburtstag* (*AOAT* 18, Neukirchen-Vluyn, 1973), pp. 65–70. On *ḥammānīm* see also Ingholt, 'Le sens du mot Ḥammān', pp. 795–802; K. Elliger, 'Der Sinn des Wortes Chammân', *ZDPV* 66 (1943), 129–39; J. Starcky, 'Autour d'une dédicace palmyrénienne à Šadrafa et à Duʿanat. 3. Le sens du mot ḤMNʾ', *Syria* 26 (1949), 51–5; W. F. Albright, *Archaeology and the Religion of Israel*, 5th edn (Garden City, 1969), pp. 216f.

26 Cf. *CIS*, no. 138, pl. XXIX (and G. Perrot and C. Chipiez, *Histoire de l'art*, vol. 3 [Paris, 1885], p. 309, fig. 232); J. I. S. Whitaker, *Motya* (London, 1921), p. 274, fig. 54; V. Karageorghis, *Cyprus* (London, 1982), pp. 147f and fig. 113.

associated with Mt. Amanus is somewhat tenuous, and other locations for El's dwelling have been suggested.[27] With regard to the alleged parallelism between the names Baal-ṣemed, Baal-ḥamman and Rakkab-El on the one hand and Hadad, El and Rakkab-El on the other, and the resulting conclusion that Baal-ḥammon = El, it may be said that there is no proof of this and that it is more probable that Baal-ṣemed and Baal-ḥamman are two different manifestations of Baal-Hadad, as their names suggest.

The final point to be considered is Baal-ḥammon's equation with Kronos. This by no means overturns the internal Punic evidence that Baal-ḥammon was Baal, for we have ancient testimony to the fact that Kronos (Saturn) could denote Baal as well as El. Thus, Servius Grammaticus, in his commentary on Virgil's *Aeneid* I, 729 declares, 'Saturn . . . in the Punic language the god is called Bal', and in Theodoret of Cyrrhus' commentary on Ps. 105.28–9, we read of 'Baal . . . They say that he is called Kronos in the Greek language'. Moreover, in Damascius' *Life of Isidorus* 115 we read that 'the Phoenicians and Syrians called Kronos El and Bel and Bolathen'. Further, it is interesting to read in Theophilus of Antioch's *Ad Autolycum* III, 29:

Moreover, since Kronos and Belos are contemporaries, the majority do not know how to distinguish Kronos and Belos. Some offer worship to Kronos giving him the name of Bel or Bal, above all the inhabitants of the Levant; but they neither know who Kronos is nor who Belos is. The Romans name him Saturn; but they do not even know which of them he is, whether Kronos or Belos.

Moreover, there is evidence that Baal-ḥammon was also equated with Zeus (the usual equivalent of Baal), since in Hannibal's oath in his treaty with Philip V of Macedon, as recorded in Polybius VII, 9, 2–3, Hannibal calls the leading Punic deities to witness the oath and Zeus comes first, but Kronos is not mentioned at all. By virtue of position it is natural to suppose that Zeus represents the chief Carthaginian god, Baal-ḥammon. Hannibal declares:

In the presence of Zeus, Hera, and Apollo; in the presence of the Genius (*daimon*) of Carthage, of Heracles, and Iolaus; in the presence of Ares, Triton, Poseidon; in the presence of the gods who battle for us and of the Sun, Moon, and Earth; in the presence of Rivers, Lakes, and Waters; in the

27 Cf. my brief discussion of the views of F. M. Cross, M. H. Pope and E. Lipiński on the location of El's dwelling in my book *God's Conflict with the Dragon and the Sea: Echoes of a Canaanite Myth in the Old Testament* (Cambridge, 1985), p. 119, n. 120.

presence of all the gods who possess Carthage; in the presence of all the gods who possess Macedonia and the rest of Greece; in the presence of all the gods of the army who preside over this oath . . .

The result of all this is that it is simply not the case that the common equation of Baal-ḥammon with Kronos in classical sources indicates that Baal-ḥammon was equivalent to El. The situation was much more complex than this as the above citations show. It may be, as W. W. Graf von Baudissin and J. G. Février have suggested[28] (cf. too Diodorus Siculus XX, 14, 7 and Tertullian, *Apology*, 9), that it was Kronos' devouring of his own children which encouraged his equation with Baal-ḥammon, the god of human sacrifice.

In conclusion, then, it may be stated that Baal-ḥammon is almost certainly a form of Baal and not El. The strongest argument is that he is often simply called Baal, whereas he is never called El.

Mot

Another view that has been put forward is that Molech is to be equated with the Canaanite god Mot, well known from the Ugaritic texts as the lord of the underworld and the summer season. This has been suggested by M. Lehmann[29] and followed by M. J. Mulder.[30] Lehmann believed that the human sacrifices offered to Molech were a dramatization of Anat's killing of Mot (cf. *CTA* 6.II.30ff=*KTU* 1.6.II.30ff). He notes that the Hebrew word *š*^{e}*ḏēmōṯ* (generally translated 'fields' or 'terraces') is associated with the Kidron valley in 2 Kgs. 23.4 and Jer. 31.40. *Š*^{e}*ḏēmōṯ*, according to Lehmann, means 'field of Mot', and since the Kidron valley was an extension of the Hinnom valley,[31] where the Molech sacrifices took place, he believes that there are grounds for equating Molech with Mot. However, both elements of the argument are hypothetical, so that the equation is improbable. First, it seems illegitimate to suppose that the Molech cult, which the Old Testament constantly associates with the valley of Hinnom, was also connected with the valley of Kidron. Although the two valleys meet they are unlikely to be regarded as the same valley. Secondly, whatever the meaning of *š*^{e}*ḏēmōṯ*, it is unlikely to be 'field

28 W. W. F. Graf von Baudissin, 'Baal und Bel' in A. Hauck (ed.), *Realencyklopädie für protestantische Theologie und Kirche*, vol. 2, 3rd edn (Leipzig, 1897), p. 333; J.-G. Février, 'Essai de reconstruction du sacrifice molek', *JA* 248 (1960), 173.
29 'A new interpretation of the term שדמות', *VT* 3 (1953), 361–71.
30 *Kanaänitische goden in het Oude Testament* (The Hague, 1965), pp. 68–70.
31 Cf. below, ch. 3, pp. 52–3, n. 89, for criticism of J. Maxwell Miller's novel views on the location of the Hinnom valley.

of Mot', since if the first element were 'field', it should be *śd* not *šd* (cf. Hebrew *śāḏeh* 'field'). It is usually supposed that the singular form of the word is *šᵉḏēmāh*, the etymology being unknown.

A more general argument against equating Molech with Mot is that we should expect the Old Testament to refer to him as Mot if this were the god in question. The Ugaritic texts never refer to Mot as *mlk*, although his kingship is once referred to (*CTA* 6.VI.28 = *KTU* 1.6.VI.28) and his throne is mentioned three times (*CTA* 4.VIII.12; 5.II.15; 6.VI.28 = *KTU* 1.4.VIII.8; 1.5.II.15; 1.6.VI.28). But other gods were described as king too, especially El and Baal, so that there was no reason for Mot to be specially singled out by this epithet. Everything suggests that *mlk* was the actual name of the god to whom human sacrifice was offered, since there was every reason for the Old Testament to avoid using *mlk* as the epithet of any god but Yahweh, as the word, which means 'king', might appear to question Yahweh's sovereignty. It is consistent with this that the Massoretes felt constrained to bowdlerize the name (presumably originally Melek) to Molech, with the vowels of the word *bōšeṯ* 'shame'.[32]

It is true, as we shall see later, that there are indications that Molech was indeed an underworld deity – points strangely not noted by the upholders of the Mot hypothesis. However, since we shall also find that there was an underworld deity actually called *mlk* (Malik), the underworld character of Molech does not necessitate his equation with Mot.

Adad-milki

A number of scholars, including K. Deller,[33] M. Weinfeld,[34] and M. Cogan,[35] want to identify Old Testament Molech with a deity Adad-milki allegedly mentioned in certain Neo-Assyrian legal contracts from the ninth to seventh centuries B.C., where one of the penalties is that a son should be burnt before Adad-milki. The element -milki would then correspond to the name Molech. We find the following five formulations:[36]

32 Cf. below, pp. 56–8.
33 Review of R. de Vaux, *Les Sacrifices de l'Ancien Testament, Orientalia* 34, NS (1965), pp. 382–6.
34 'The worship of Molech and of the Queen of Heaven and its background', *UF* 4 (1972), 144–9.
35 *Imperialism and Religion* (Missoula, 1974), pp. 81–3.
36 The translations here follow those in Weinfeld, 'The worship of Molech', pp. 144f. The original places of publication are as follows: (i) in C. H. W. Johns, *Assyrian Deeds and Documents*, vol. 1 (Cambridge, 1898), p. 488, no. 632 = J. Kohler and A.

(i) His eldest son will be burnt in the *ḫamru* of the god Adad.

(ii) His son he will burn to Adad-milki, his eldest daughter, together with two *se'ahs* of cedar resin, he will burn to Bēlet-ṣēri.

(iii) His eldest son or his eldest daughter, together with two *homers* of good spice, he will burn to Bēlet-ṣēri.

(iv) His eldest son he will burn before Adad-milki, his eldest daughter he will burn before Bēlet-ṣēri . . . He will hand over seven priests and seven priestesses to Adad, who dwells in Kurbail, and will give seven sacred male prostitutes and seven sacred female prostitutes to Ishtar, who dwells in Arbail.

(v) His seven sons he will burn before Adad and his seven daughters he will lead forth as sacred prostitutes to Ishtar.

Interestingly, as with the Old Testament references to burning to Molech, there has been a certain amount of discussion whether actual burning is intended or whether this is simply a metaphor for dedication – here to the priesthood of the deity. Cogan[37] and Morton Smith[38] have taken the former view and Johns,[39] Deller[40] and Weinfeld[41] the latter. As Smith[42] has forcefully expressed it, however, 'we may plausibly presume the texts mean what they say'. If 'to be burned' meant 'to be made a priest or prostitute', we should expect the same language to be used of both groups in (iv) and (v) and the fact that it is not strongly suggests that these are different things.

Do these texts then justify our equating Molech with Adad-milki? Although this may at first seem attractive, it is now certain that this view should be rejected. First, the deity in question would be

Ungnad, *Assyrische Rechtsurkunden* (Leipzig, 1913), p. 122, no. 160:8, and Johns, *Assyrian Deeds*, vol. 2 (Cambridge, 1901), p. 58, no. 805 = Kohler and Ungnad, *Assyrische Rechtsurkunden*, p. 122, no. 161:2; there are also a number of other examples, cf. the references in Deller, *Les Sacrifices*, p. 383; (ii) in Johns, *Assyrian Deeds*, vol. 1, pp. 351f, no. 436 r. 7–9 = Kohler and Ungnad, *Assyrische Rechtsurkunden*, p. 124, no. 163:20–22, and Johns, *Assyrian Deeds*, vol. 1, p. 390, no. 474 r. 3–6 = Kohler and Ungnad, *Assyrische Rechtsurkunden*, p. 76, no. 96a:16–18; (iii) in Johns, *Assyrian Deeds*, vol. 1, p. 228, no. 310 r. 7–10 = Kohler and Ungnad, *Assyrische Rechtsurkunden*, p. 120, no. 158:27–30, following the collation of J. N. Postgate (cf. Weinfeld, 'The worship of Molech', p. 144, n. 88); (iv) in D. J. Wiseman and J. V. Kinnier Wilson, 'The Nimrud tablets, 1950', *Iraq* 13 (1951), 117 and pl. XVI, ND 496:25–32; (v) in B. Meissner, 'Die Keilschrifttexte auf den steinernen Orthostaten und Statuen aus dem Tell Ḥalâf', *Aus fünf Jahrtausenden morgenländischer Kultur. Festschrift Max Freiherrn von Oppenheim zum 70 Geburtstage* (*Archiv für Orientforschung Beiheft* 1, Berlin, 1933), p. 73, no. 8:5–7.

37 *Imperialism*, p. 83 and n. 98.

38 'A note on burning babies', *JAOS* 95 (1975), p. 479.

39 Johns, *Assyrian Deeds*, vol. 3 (Cambridge, 1901), pp. 345f.

40 *Les Sacrifices*, p. 385.

41 'The worship of Molech', p. 145.

42 'A note on burning babies', p. 479.

Aramean in origin, whereas the Old Testament gives many indications that the Molech cult is Canaanite. Secondly, one might ask, if the deity to whom human sacrifice was offered in Israel was Adad-milki, why is he called Molech rather than (H)adad-melek in the Old Testament? The Old Testament is not in the habit of referring to other deities by falsely abbreviated names. Thirdly, burning to Molech was not a punishment, unlike the cases cited above. Fourthly, and most significantly, it should be noted that S. A. Kaufman[43] has fairly recently seriously questioned whether the name of the deity should be read as Adad-milki at all. The most fundamental argument is that the sign ^{d}XXX (divided by Deller into U.MAN = Adad-milki) normally denotes the god Sin. W. G. Lambert, in a private communication (dated 11 February 1982), emphasizes that 'since ^{d}XXX is so common for Sin, one suspects that scribes of administrative and economic documents would not also use it for Adad-milki'. To return to Kaufman, he also notes that the word *ḫamru* 'precinct' mentioned in the cases involving Adad is never found in connection with the alleged occurrences of Adad-milki, suggesting that they are different deities, and this is further supported by the fact that in one case ^{d}XXX is mentioned alongside Adad (of Arbail) as if they were separate gods.[44] Although there is more evidence for the actual existence of a god Adad-milki in other texts than Kaufman allows,[45] it is clear that he is not mentioned in these legal contracts in connection with burning human beings, and that these are therefore not the place where the background of the Molech cult is to be sought.

43 'The enigmatic Adad-milki', *JNES* 37 (1978), 101–9, esp. 107.

44 *Ibid.*, p. 107, also claims that in one instance the sign SIG occurs after ^{d}XXX, which has the phonetic value *si* (or *siʾ*) in Neo-Assyrian, showing that ^{d}XXX is to be read *Siʾ*, the Aramaic form of the name of the god Sin. However, Lambert in his letter rejects this particular argument, because 'in addition to the problem that it (*sc.* SIG) does not seem to occur in Late Assyrian tablets, and only once in Late Babylonian, one does not use rare signs to gloss others!'

45 *Ibid.*, pp. 103f, proposes to read a number of personal names which Deller had understood as containing the elements Adad-milki as rather including the elements Adad-iški. However, Lambert writes in his letter:

'I side with Deller against Kaufman and von Soden in not inclining to read iš-ki. "Testicle" can be understood as a metaphor for "son", and its occurrence in the synonym list Malku = šarru supports it as a literary usage. Such literary rarities are the backbone of the list and I do not find a single personal name where iški is sure, or even probable. Kaufman's argument that by reading Adad-Milki-ʿēʾreš etc. one is at a loss to explain why no case of e.g. Adad-Milki-zēra-ʿēʾreš occurs, is unacceptable. On one of the lists used, *Iraq* 16, pp. 47ff, I find the names Marduk-ʿēʾreš and Marduk-(i)rība, so there is no problem of lack of object in this type of name. The question overlooked by Kaufman is that the Akkadian lexica do not accept milku 'king', though his quotation of Sîn-mil-ki-ilī certainly appears to be

It thus appears that although there is some evidence for the existence of a god Adad-milki, it is not as extensive as was previously thought, but in any case, there is no evidence from Akkadian sources that he was worshipped with rites of human sacrifice. Is it the case, however, that there is evidence of this in 2 Kgs. 17.31? This verse is part of a section giving details of various peoples whom the Assyrians settled in Samaria after 722 B.C., together with a note about their religion, and as the MT stands we read that 'the Sepharvites burned their children in the fire to Adrammelech[46] and Anammelech, the gods of Sepharvaim'. The suggestion was apparently first made by P. Jensen[47] and has been followed by a considerable number of scholars subsequently,[48] that we should emend Adrammelech to Adadmelech, which would then be equivalent to Akkadian Adad-milki. The emendation of ר to ד is certainly an easy one (even though it has no versional support), since the confusion of these two letters in the Hebrew Bible is well attested. It has, moreover, a certain attraction in view of the fact that Sepharvaim seems to have been somewhere in the area of Syria,[49] where Hadad was the leading deity.

There is, however, good reason to believe that this emendation is mistaken and in favour of continuing to read with the MT Adrammelech. We should more naturally expect Hadadmelech rather than Adadmelech, since the storm deity is regularly called Hadad, not Adad, in the Old Testament. This is clearly not a

an example, and that is Middle Babylonian in date, too early for Aramaic influence. However, assuming that the lexica are in general correct, one must then take Adad-Milki (or however else one may choose to read d.IM or U) as Aramaic. There is of course, *pace* Kaufman, no problem in a personal name with Aramaic divine name and Akkadian verb. The ancients were not tied to our linguistic susceptibilities. The names with, by this reading, Adad-Milki are not common, and are spread far: Nineveh, Assur, Nimrud, Gozan, Nippur. But they are few at each place.'

46 Adrammelech also occurs in 2 Kgs. 19.37 as the name of one of the sons of Sennacherib who murdered him. The name of this individual in cuneiform is now known to have been Arda-Mulišši, cf. S. Parpola, 'The murderer of Sennacherib' in B. Alster (ed.), *Mesopotamia 8. Death in Mesopotamia. Papers Read at the XXVIe Rencontre Assyriologique Internationale* (Copenhagen, 1980), pp. 171–82. He occurs similarly as Adramelos in Abydenus' version of Berossus. It is therefore possible that the name in 2 Kgs. 19.37 was originally Adrammelesh and that this may have been corrupted to Adrammelech through the influence of the name in 2 Kgs. 17.31.

47 Review of H. V. Hilprecht (ed.), *The Babylonian Expedition of the University of Pennsylvania, Zeitschrift für Assyriologie* 13 (1898), 333, n. 1.

48 A. Ungnad in J. Friedrich, G. R. Meyer, A. Ungnad, E. F. Weidner (eds.), *Die Inschriften vom Tell Halaf* (*Archiv für Orientforschung Beiheft* 6, Berlin, 1940), p. 58; A. Pohl, 'Miszellen', *Biblica* 22 (1941), 35; Albright, *Archaeology and the Religion of Israel*, pp. 157f, and others.

49 Cf. below, p. 46.

conclusive argument, however, since the form Adad does occur as a variant of the name Hadad the Edomite in 1 Kgs. 11.17.[50] What is interesting, however, and suggests that the emendation of Adrammelech to Adadmelech is unnecessary, is that the form Adrammelech actually occurs as the name of a king of Byblos in Phoenicia in the fourth century B.C.[51] This suggests that the name is Phoenician. The name seems to occur in Plutarch, *De Iside et Osiride*, 15 as Malkandros, whose son was burnt by the goddess Isis (16).[52] As J. Ebach and U. Rüterswörden have pointed out,[53] there may be some connection here with Adrammelech as a god of human sacrifice. The name Anammelech is also perhaps best explained as Phoenician or Canaanite, as Kaufman[54] has suggested, since An occurs as the masculine form of the divine name Anat in Ugaritic and Phoenician texts.[55] Alternatively, it is possible that Anammelech denotes Anatmelech (Anat of Melech).[56] Either of these suggestions seems preferable to seeing it as containing the name of the Mesopotamian god Anu,[57] which is unlikely because fiery human sacrifice seems to be virtually unattested in Mesopotamia as a form of worship.[58]

50 Note too S. A. Kaufman, 'An Assyro-Aramaic *egirtu ša šulmu*' in M. de Jong Ellis (ed.), *Essays on the Ancient Near East in Memory of Jacob Joel Finkelstein* (Hamden, 1977), p. 123, for evidence of *ʾad* (though not *ʾadad*) as an Aramaic form of the name of the god Hadad.

51 Cf. G. F. Hill, *Catalogue of the Greek Coins of Phoenicia* (London, 1910), p. 96; M. Dunand, *Fouilles de Byblos*, vol. 1 (Paris, 1939), p. 407.

52 Not Malkandros himself, as stated by T. H. Gaster, *Myth, Legend, and Custom in the Old Testament* (London, 1969), p. 587. That the name Malkandros derives from *mlk ʾadr* has been held by J. Friedrich and W. Röllig, *Phönizisch-Punische Grammatik*, 2nd edn (Rome, 1970), §58c, n. 2; J. Ebach and U. Rüterswörden, 'ADRMLK, "Moloch" und BA^C^AL ADR', *UF* 11 (1979), 224. J. Gwyn Griffiths, *Plutarch's De Iside et Osiride* (Cardiff, 1970), p. 142, n. 1, however, emends *Μάλκανδρον* to *Μάλκαθρον* (Melqart). See too his note on p. 325.

53 'ADRMLK', pp. 224–6.

54 'Adad-milki', pp. 102–3, n. 9. If one adopts this view one should perhaps emend Anammelech to Anmelech.

55 Cf. J. T. Milik, 'An unpublished arrow-head with Phoenician inscription of the 11th–10th century B.C.', *BASOR* 143 (1956), 3–6; *KAI* 22 Rs; H. B. Huffmon, *Amorite Personal Names in the Mari Texts* (Baltimore, 1965), p. 199; M. Dahood, *Ugaritic–Hebrew Philology* (Rome, 1965), p. 67; F. Gröndahl, *Die Personennamen der Texte aus Ugarit* (Rome, 1967), pp. 83, 110.

56 Cf. R. Kittel, *Geschichte des Volkes Israel*, 5th and 6th edns (Gotha, 1923–5), p. 181, n. 4; O. Eissfeldt, 'Adrammelek und Demarus', *Annuaire de l'Institut de Philologie et d'Histoire Orientales et Slaves*, 13 (1953), p. 159, reprinted in *Kleine Schriften* 3 (Tübingen, 1966), 339; Weinfeld, 'The worship of Molech', p. 149.

57 E.g. Albright, *Archaeology and the Religion of Israel*, pp. 157f. In an earlier study 'The evolution of the West-Semitic divinity ʿAn-ʿAnat-ʿAtta', *AJSL* 41 (1925), 86f, Albright suggested that Anammelech was a fusion of the Mesopotamian god Anu and the Syrian god An.

58 See Heider, *The Cult of Molek*, pp. 204–10, for a discussion of the sparse nature of the evidence for human sacrifice in Mesopotamia.

Sepharvaim is probably to be sought in Syria. This is suggested by the fact that it is mentioned after Hamath and Arpad in both 2 Kgs. 18.34 and 19.13 (cf. too Hamath in 2 Kgs. 17.30, two names before Sepharvaim in v. 31). It may well be identical with Sibraim, mentioned in Ezek. 47.16 as lying on the border between Damascus and Hamath.[59] The older view equating Sepharvaim with Sippar in Mesopotamia[60] is now generally given up. G. R. Driver[61] attempted to revive it, also equating the Hamath of 2 Kgs. 17.30 with *mat A-ma-ti* in Elam, but this is unconvincing, since this Hamath can hardly be separated from the Hamath of 2 Kgs. 18.34 and 19.13 which is mentioned alongside Arpad (in Syria). Furthermore, he has problems with Ashima, the deity of Hamath, which he admits is Syrian in form. The mention of Hamath also makes M. C. Astour's location of Sepharvaim in Media improbable.[62]

Molech as an underworld god

Molech = Ugaritic mlk = Akkadian Malik

We have seen from the above that it is unlikely that Molech conceals the name of some other deity with a different name. It is most natural to suppose that a specific deity Molech is in mind or, if as seems likely, the name has been inserted with the vowels of *bōšeṯ* 'shame',[63] a deity called Melek. The fact that the god is constantly called by this name suggests that it is not simply an epithet 'the king', but the actual name of the deity in question. The fact that it is constantly preceded by the definite article does not indicate otherwise,[64] since this is likewise the case with Baal, which though in origin an epithet ('lord') for the god Hadad, certainly serves as a proper name of the deity. In both instances a common noun has come to be treated as virtually a proper name (like 'the Lord' in English), but it has not ceased to have its earlier meaning.

Was there a deity in the West Semitic world whose name could be rendered Molech or Melek in the Old Testament? Indeed there was. That a god *mlk* was known among the Canaanites is proved by two Ugaritic texts, both of which are serpent charms, and which are

59 Cf. Albright, *Archaeology and the Religion of Israel*, p. 222, n. 116.
60 E.g. F. Delitzsch, *Wo lag das Paradies?* (Leipzig, 1881), p. 211.
61 'Geographical problems', *Eretz-Israel* 5 (Jerusalem, 1958), 18*–20*.
62 'Sepharvaim', *The Interpreter's Dictionary of the Bible Supplementary Volume* (Nashville, 1976), p. 807. 63 Cf. below, pp. 56–8.
64 *Contra* H. H. Rowley, review of K. Dronkert, *De Molochdienst in het Oude Testament* (Leiden, 1953), *Bibliotheca Orientalis* 10 (1953), cols. 195–6.

published in *Ugaritica* V. They are *Ugaritica* V. 7 (*RS* 24.244 = *KTU* 1.100), line 41 and *Ugaritica* V. 8 (*RS* 24.251 = *KTU* 1.107),line 17.[65] The former reference has *mlk ʿṯtrth* and the latter has *mlk bʿṯtrt*. In both serpent charm texts these allusions come as one of a series of divine names. That *ʿṯtrth* is a place name 'in Ashtaroth', and not simply a reference to the well-known goddess Astarte, is proved by the fact that other gods are mentioned together with their cult place, indicated likewise with locative *h*, for example *kṯr . wḫss . kptrh* 'Kothar-and-Ḫasis in Crete' (line 46), *dgn. ttlh* 'Dagan in Tuttul' (line 15), etc.[66] The parallel allusion to *mlk bʿṯtrt* must similarly allude to '*mlk* in Ashtaroth', as the parallelism between the two texts in the matter of deities is very clear. Presumably Ashtaroth is the place in Bashan mentioned by this name in the Old Testament (cf. Deut. 1.4; Josh. 9.10, 12.4, 13.12, 31), the site of which is at Tell 'Ashtarah. The Transjordanian location makes it possible that there was originally a connection with Milcom, the god of the Ammonites, even though in the Old Testament they are clearly distinct deities. Anyway, the important point for our purpose is that we have here irrefutable evidence that there was a Canaanite god *mlk*, which is precisely what the Old Testament allusions to Molech seem to demand.

This deity is also attested more widely throughout the Syrian and Mesopotamian regions. For example, he appears as Malik in various god lists[67] and in personal names from Ebla, Mari, and Ugarit.[68] Although in some of the personal names *malik* or *mlk* is clearly an epithet of some other god, there are some cases where it is clearly a

65 On the first of these texts, see for example D. Pardee, 'A philological and prosodic analysis of the Ugaritic serpent incantation *UT* 607', *JANESCU* 10 (1978), 73–108.

66 S. Ribichini, 'Un 'ipotesi per Milkʿaštart', *RSO* 50 (1976), p. 48, prefers to think that we have here a reference to *mlk* in association with the goddess Astarte, but this seems forced in view of the parallels to which I have drawn attention.

67 In addition to the references cited below in nn. 70, 72, and 73, the following is a list of some of the other occurrences of Malik: K. F. Müller, *Das assyrische Ritual: 1. Texte zum assyrischen Königsritual* (Leipzig, 1937), pp. 16–17, line 19; R. Frankena, *Tākultu, de sacrale maaltijd in het Assyrische ritueel* (Leiden, 1953), p. 5, col. 2, line 9, and p. 25, line 16; B. Menzel, *Assyrische Tempel*, vol. 2 (Rome, 1981), p. T129, text 58, line 59, p. T130, text 58, vs., line 29, and p. T148, text 64, line 32 A and B.

68 A list of Eblaite personal names containing the element *ma-lik* may be found in Heider, *The Cult of Molek*, pp. 409–15 (and see discussion on pp. 96–100). Three of the names contain the divine determinative: Dar-^{d}ma-lik, Bù-AN-ma-lik, and Ìr-^{d}ma-lik. It should be noted, though, that the first two names occur only once each and the last, which occurs frequently, could also be read Ìr-an-ma-lik. That *ma-lik* certainly does occur as a divine name at Ebla is shown by the fact that personal names containing the element *ma-lik* are closely paralleled by other

divine name. Amongst the Amorites at Mari, in addition to the Maliku, who appear as underworld deities receiving sacrifices for the dead along with Dagan in the Kispum ritual (appearing at Ugarit in a bilingual Akkadian–Ugaritic god list [*RS* 20.24, *Ugaritica* V. 18] as ^{d}MA.LIK.MEŠ = *mlkm*),[69] there was also a deity ^{d}*Ma-lik šarru ša Má-ri*^{ki} 'Malik king of Mari'.[70] That he was also known as Muluk at Mari is indicated by the place name variously spelled I-lu-um-Mu-lu-uk^{ki}, DINGIR-Mu-lu-uk-^{ki}, DINGIR-Mu-lu-ka-wi^{ki} and I-lu-Ma-li-ka-wi^{ki}.[71]

What is important for our purpose is that Malik is equated with Nergal, the Mesopotamian underworld god, in two texts, once in a list of gods from the Old Babylonian period, where we find ^{d}Ma-lik = ^{d}Nergal,[72] and again later in a god list from Ashur,[73] where we

personal names containing the names of known deities: one may compare I-ti-ma-lik with I-ti-^{d}Enki and I-ti-^{d}Ra-sa-ap, En-na-ma-lik with En-na-^{d}Utu and En-na-$^{(d)}$Da-gan, and Bù-da-Ba-al and Bù-da-Il. For a list of Mari personal names containing the element *mlk*, see *ibid.*, pp. 416f (and discussion on pp. 103–7), which is based on I. J. Gelb, *Computer-aided Analysis of Amorite* (Chicago, 1980), which in turn has a complete list including names in both Huffmon, *Amorite Personal Names*, and G. Buccellati, *The Amorites of the Ur III Period* (Naples, 1966). As at Ebla, it is not always possible to know whether *mlk* is the name of a god or the epithet of some other god. It was clearly sometimes the latter (e.g. in ^{d}Na-bu-ú-ma-lik), but it was also clearly sometimes an actual divine name, as when *ma-lik* contains the divine determinative (cf. Ia-šu-ub-^{d} ma-[lik]) and probably when *ma-lik* occurs in names paralleled by other theophorous names, e.g. in Ḫa-ab-du-ma-lik (cf. Ḫabdu-Ištar). For a list of personal names containing the element *mlk* at Ugarit, cf. Heider, *The Cult of Molek*, pp. 418f (and discussion on pp. 133–7), in addition to Gröndahl, *Die Personennamen*, pp. 84, 157. In some instances *mlk* is clearly the epithet of some other god (e.g. Kṯrmlk), but in one case *ma-lik* occurs in a personal name with the divine determinative (Nûrī-^{d}ma-lik) and in others *mlk* occupies the place which in others have a known divine name (cf. ʾAbmlk and ʾAbrpʾu).

69 Cf. J. F. Healey, '*Malkū: mlkm: Anunnaki*', *UF* 7 (1975), 235–8.

70 Cf. II R 60, i, 20, in E. Ebeling, *Tod und Leben nach den Vorstellungen der Babylonier. 1. Texte* (Berlin and Leipzig, 1931), p. 12.

71 Cf. J. Bottéro and A. Finet (eds.), *Archives Royales de Mari*, vol. 15 (Paris, 1954), p. 127. See also G. Dossin, 'Signaux lu eux au pays de Mari', *RA* 35 (1938), 178, n. 1.

72 Cf. S. Langdon (ed.), *The H. Weld-Blundell Collection in the Ashmolean Museum. Vol. 1. Sumerian and Semitic Religious and Historical Texts*, Oxford editions of cuneiform texts, vol. 1 (Oxford, 1923), p. 31, text 9, obv. col. 2, line 8.

73 Cf. O. Schroeder, *Keilschrifttexte aus Assur verschiedenen Inhalts* (Leipzig, 1920), 63.II.37; K. Tallqvist, *Akkadische Götterepitheta* (Helsinki, 1938), p. 359. According to W. G. Lambert, 'Götterlisten' in E. Weidner and W. von Soden (eds.), *Reallexikon der Assyriologie*, vol. 3 (Berlin and New York, 1957–71), p. 474a, this text is Late Assyrian in date. However, this text is not included in Menzel, *Assyrische Tempel*, presumably on the assumption that it is Middle Assyrian.

likewise find ^{d}Ma-lik = ^{d}Nergal.[74] This clearly indicates that Malik was an underworld deity. Furthermore, it tends to support his identity with the Molech of the Old Testament, since, as we shall now see, there is evidence indicating that Molech was an underworld god.

It is conceivable that Malik is the same as the Phoenician god Melqart, whose name is commonly analysed as consisting of *mlk* + *qrt* 'king of the city'. Albright[75] took this to mean 'king of the (underworld) city' but usually it is understood to mean 'king of the city (of Tyre)', whose god Melqart was.[76] We do not possess sufficient ancient material about Melqart, however, to come to a decisive judgment on this question. Nevertheless, there is evidence from Palmyra that Melqart was equated with Nergal,[77] the underworld god, which might suggest a relationship with Molech. However, in our current state of knowledge (or rather ignorance) with regard to Melqart, it seems best to keep an open mind on this question and await further evidence.[78]

The case for the underworld nature of the Ugaritic god *mlk* would receive further support if one were to follow the view of M. H. Pope and G. C. Heider,[79] according to which *mlk* is to be equated with *rpʾu*. Following a similar proposal of B. Margulis (Margalit),[80] Pope renders *Ugaritica* V. 2 (*RS* 24.252 = *KTU* 1.108), lines 2–3, *ʾil. yṯb. bʿṯtrt ʾil ṯpṭ. bhd rʿy* as 'the god who dwells in Ashtaroth, the god who

74 It should perhaps be noted at this point that the standard equivalent of Nergal is Resheph. Thus, for Ugarit, cf. the god lists *CTA* 29 (= *KTU* 1.47) and *RS* 24.264 + 24.280 (= *KTU* 1.118) = *RS* 20.24 (line 26), in *Ugaritica* V (Paris, 1968), p. 45, and *Ugaritica* VII (Paris, 1978), p. 3.

75 *Archaeology and the Religion of Israel*, p. 79.

76 E.g. G. Levi della Vida, 'Some notes on the stele of Ben-Hadad', *BASOR* 90 (1943), 30, n. 2.

77 Cf. H. Seyrig, 'Antiquités syriennes. Héraclès-Nergal', *Syria* 24 (1944–5), 62–80.

78 With regard to Melqart the old works of F. C. Movers, *Die Phönizier*, vol. 1 (Bonn, 1841), pp. 177f, 385–414, and D. Raoul-Rochette, *Mémoires d'Archéologie comparée, asiatique, grecque et étrusque. Premier Mémoire sur l'Hercule assyrien et phénicien, considéré dans ses rapports avec l'Hercule grec* (Paris, 1848), are still valuable for their citations from classical sources, even though in other ways they are dated. More recent works are R. de Vaux, 'Les Prophètes de Baal sur le Mont Carmel', *Bulletin du Musée de Beyrouth* 5 (1941), 7–20, reprinted in his book *Bible et Orient* (Paris, 1967), pp. 485–97 (ET, *The Bible and the Ancient Near East* [Garden City, 1971], pp. 238–51); E. Lipiński, 'La fête de l'ensevelissement et de la résurrection de Melqart', *Actes de la XVIIe Rencontre Assyriologique Internationale* (Ham-sur-Heure, 1970), 30–58; C. Bonnet, *Melqart* (Studia Phoenicia 8, Louvain, 1988).

79 M. H. Pope, 'Notes on the Ugaritic Rephaim texts' in M. de Jong Ellis (ed.), *Essays on the Ancient Near East in Memory of Jacob Joel Finkelstein* (Hamden, 1977), pp. 169–72; Heider, *The Cult of Molek*, pp. 115–23.

80 'A Ugaritic Psalm (RŠ 24.252)', *JBL* 89 (1970), 292–304.

rules in Edrei'. This is seen as referring to *rpʾu. mlk. ʿlm*, the deity referred to in the previous line, and following Margulis, Pope compares the Old Testament allusions to 'Og, king of Bashan, of the remnant of the Rephaim, who dwelt in Ashtaroth and Edrei' (cf. Josh. 12.4, 13.12, 31; Num. 21.33; Deut. 1.4, 3.1, 10). However, the proposed rendering of the Ugaritic text is probably to be rejected in favour of some such rendering as 'El sits with Astarte, El the judge with Hadad the shepherd', as argued, for example, by A. J. Ferrara and S. B. Parker.[81] Thus, the first letter of Edrei is ʾ, not *h*, and the relative clause which follows in the Ugaritic passage, beginning *dyšr wyḏmr bknr* 'who sings and plays on the lyre . . .', most naturally has as its antecedent the immediately preceding *hd rʿy*, which ought therefore to denote a person. It is true that elsewhere in Ugaritic *yṯb b* means 'dwell/sit in' rather than 'sit with', but in the light of the limited amount of material, this argument is not decisive. Indeed, a reference to the god (or El) dwelling in Ashtaroth and Edrei seems less appropriate in the context of this banquet scene than a reference to El (or the god) sitting with Astarte and Hadad. Accordingly, we should reject the view that the Ugaritic text speaks of *rpʾu*'s dwelling in Ashtaroth and Edrei, and the grounds for equating him with the god *mlk* who dwells in Ashtaroth in *Ugaritica* V. 7 (*RS* 24.244 = *KTU* 1.100), line 41 and *Ugaritica* V. 8 (*RS* 24.251 = *KTU* 1.107), line 17.

Isaiah 57.9

We have seen above that there was a god Malik who was equated with Nergal and who therefore seems to have been an underworld deity. That this Malik is the same as the Old Testament Molech, and that there is not simply a coincidence of names, is indicated by the fact that there is evidence that Molech was likewise an underworld god.

The most important piece of evidence is provided by Isa. 57.9, where we read: 'You journeyed to Molech (MT *meleḵ*) with oil and multiplied your perfumes; you sent your envoys far off and sent down even to Sheol.' The imagery of the journey to Sheol continues in verse 10: 'You were wearied with the length of your way, but you did not say, "it is hopeless"; you found new life for your strength,[82] and so you were not faint.' Verse 5 has already referred to rites of human sacrifice alongside the fertility cult, 'You who slay your children in

81 'Seating arrangements at divine banquets', *UF* 4 (1972), 37–9.

82 The MT here has *ḥayyaṯ yāḏēḵ*, lit. 'the life of your hand', and it is generally supposed that 'hand' is to be interpreted in the sense of 'strength'. Others emend to *dē ḥayyāṯēḵ*, translating 'you found a sufficient livelihood for yourself'.

the valleys, under the clefts of the rocks',[83] and it is natural to suppose that verse 9 is talking about the same thing. The context is quite opposed to the view, held for example by O. Eissfeldt,[84] that it is a question of an earthly, Babylonian king (*meleḵ*), since the whole passage is concerned with religious syncretism and the reference to Sheol is also inconsistent with this view. Indeed, the important point for our present purpose is this reference to Sheol,[85] since it provides evidence that Molech was an underworld deity. The parallelism of the verse makes it clear that the journeying to Molech is synonymous with the sending down to Sheol.

In this verse *tāšūrī* has been rendered above 'you journeyed', as is generally done, compare *AV*, *RV*, *RSV*, etc. This meaning for the root *šūr* appears to be found elsewhere in the Old Testament in Song of Songs 4.8 and Ezek. 27.25. Moreover, this rendering is strongly supported by verse 10, 'You were wearied with the length of *your way* . . .', which clearly means that the subject 'you' at the beginning of verse 9 is engaged in a long journey (to Sheol) and not simply the envoys of verse 9b. The common rendering 'you journeyed' therefore has strong support and it makes abundantly clear the underworld associations of the god Molech.

At this point we should note other renderings of *tāšūrī* that have been proposed. G. R. Driver[86] and later P. Wernberg-Møller[87] drew attention to the fact that at this point the LXX reads καὶ ἐπλήθυνας and the former suggested that this is based on a Hebrew verb which is cognate with the Arabic verb *ṯarra* 'abounded (with blood, milk, rain, water)'. Driver then translated verse 9, 'and

83 Cf. above, p. 16, n. 2.

84 *Molk als Opferbegriff im Punischen und Hebräischen und das Ende des Gottes Moloch* (Halle, 1935), p. 45, n. 1.

85 D. W. Thomas, 'A consideration of some unusual ways of expressing the superlative in Hebrew', *VT* 3 (1953), 223f, eliminates a reference to the underworld here by regarding *ʿaḏ-š^{e}ʾōl* as a superlative expression meaning 'to the lowest depths', maintaining that we have a reference to 'the utter debasement of the apostate Israelites before a foreign king' (p. 224). However, quite apart from the unlikeliness of a reference here to an earthly king, which does not fit the context (see above), it may be pointed out that there are no clear examples of the superlative use of *š^{e}ʾōl* anywhere in the Old Testament. The two other possibilities which Thomas cites, Song of Songs 8.6 and Ps 18.6 (ET 5), are more readily explicable on the view that we have a literal reference to the underworld, and the same is true of Isa. 57.9 (cf. the reference to human sacrifice in v. 5). Thomas's view has, indeed, gained little following.

86 'Difficult words in the Hebrew prophets' in H. H. Rowley (ed.), *Studies in Old Testament Prophecy Presented to Professor Theodore H. Robinson* (Edinburgh, 1950), pp. 58f.

87 'Two notes', *VT* 8 (1958), 307f.

thou wast drenched with oil for (=in honour of) the king . . .'.[88] Wernberg-Møller, however, suggested that the verb is cognate with Arabic *ṯarā* 'be considerable' (intr.), 'multiply' (tr.), and proposed translating 'you lavish oil on Melek . . .'. However, the LXX's translation of both the preceding and following words is so wayward that it seems unwise to seek illumination of the meaning of *tāšūrī* from this version. Thus, quite apart from a case of homoioteleuton in verse 8 (the translator's eye seems to have jumped from *hirḥaḇt miškāḇēḵ* to *ʾāhaḇt miškāḇām*) and the failure to translate *yāḏ ḥāzīṯ* at the end of the verse, we find in verse 9 that the two words following *tāšūrī* (*lammeleḵ baššemen*) seem to bear no relation to the LXX's words after ἐπλήθυνας (τὴν πορνείαν σου μετ' αὐτῶν) and later in the verse *rqḥyk* was misread as *rḥqyk* (τοὺς μακρὰν ἀπὸ σοῦ). The LXX's rendering is most unreliable at this point and it therefore seems sensible to maintain the meaning of *šūr* well attested elsewhere in the Old Testament, 'to journey'. Furthermore, as was pointed out above, the words at the beginning of verse 10, 'You were wearied with the length of *your way*' as well as 'you sent . . . and sent down' in verse 9 tend to support the translation 'you journeyed'.
journeyed'.

The fundamental contribution of Isa. 57.9 which I wish to emphasize, however, is the evidence it provides for Molech's association with the underworld, thus agreeing with Malik, who was equated with Nergal.

The fires of Molech and Gehenna

It is well known that Gehenna is a term for hell in Jewish literature and the New Testament (e.g. 2 Esdras 7.36; 2 Baruch 59.10, 85.13; Mark 9.43, 45, 47) and that Gehenna derives from the Aramaic name for the valley of Hinnom, Gehinnam, the valley to the south-east of Old Testament Jerusalem.[89] As a term for hell Gehenna is constantly

88 Earlier, in 'Studies in the vocabulary of the Old Testament. VII', *JTS* 35 (1934), 389, Driver had proposed connecting *tāšūrī* with Akkadian *šarāru* 'to be resplendent' and Arabic *sarra*, and rendered the passage 'and thou wast glistening with oil before the king'. In his 1950 article, however, he seems to prefer his new proposal because of the support which he finds for it in the LXX (p. 58).

89 This localization of the valley of Hinnom is universally accepted, with the single exception of J. Maxwell Miller, 'Jebus and Jerusalem: a case of mistaken identity', *ZDPV* 90 (1974), 115–27. He claims that Jebus was originally a village several miles north of Jerusalem, at the place now called Shaʿfat, and holds that the equation of Jebus or 'the Jebusite' with Jerusalem in the Old Testament is not only secondary but false (cf. Josh. 15.8, 18.16, 28, 19.10; Judg. 19.10; 1 Chron. 11.4). Since the valley of Hinnom is mentioned as being adjacent to 'the Jebusite' in the Joshua passages cited, Miller has to claim that this likewise was several miles to

associated with fires which bring punishment to the wicked. What is the origin of this concept? There is a popular notion that Gehenna became a term for hell because there was a garbage heap there which was constantly being burnt up by an incinerator and that corpses were thrown on to it. However, besides the fact that cremation does not seem to have been usual,[90] there is no archaeological support for this view and no ancient writer attests it. It is found for the first time only about A.D. 1200 in Ḳimḥi's commentary on Ps. 27.13: 'And it [*sc.* Gehenna] was a despised place where they cast filth and corpses, and there was there perpetually a fire for the burning of the filth and the bones of the corpses. On account of this the judgment place of the wicked is parabolically called Gehenna.'[91]

The only fires that are certainly attested in connection with the valley of Hinnom are those associated with the sacrifices offered to the god Molech. If Molech was indeed an underworld deity, we have

the North. He maintains that it is the modern Wadi Beit Ḥanina, even claiming that the name Hinnom is still echoed in Ḥanina, but the fact that the Hebrew has *h* and the Arabic *ḥ* tells against this. Moreover, not only was later Jewish tradition confident in placing the Hinnom valley next to Jerusalem (e.g. 1 Enoch 27.1, cf. 26.1ff), but the Old Testament itself is unanimous in so placing it. In Jer. 19.2 the valley of Hinnom is immediately outside Jerusalem and in Jer. 31.40 the Kidron valley by Jerusalem is connected to 'the whole valley of the dead bodies and the ashes', which is surely an allusion to the Hinnom valley with its human sacrificial cult. Miller fails to discuss the latter passage but claims that the former is part of a secondary insertion in Jer. 19. However this may be, there is no doubt that both these passages are evidence of the equation of the Hinnom valley with a valley adjacent to Jerusalem in the Old Testament period. Since Jerusalem was at the centre of the nation's life and consciousness, it seems inherently implausible that the valley immediately outside it should have been confused with another one several miles to the North, already in Old Testament times. It is more natural to suppose that the valley by Jerusalem really was the Hinnom valley.

As far as Jebus is concerned, Miller's arguments that this is not Jerusalem are also unconvincing. See H. Y. Priebatsch, 'Jerusalem und die Brunnenstrasse Merneptahs', *ZDPV* 9 (1975), 24–9. In addition to Priebatsch's arguments I would note the following point. Miller objected that if Jebus in the Joshua passage meant Jerusalem, Jerusalem would be in Benjamin, whereas we know it to have been in Judah in reality. Against this, however, I would draw attention to Jer. 6.1, 'Flee for safety, O people of Benjamin, from the midst of Jerusalem!', which makes it clear that Jerusalem could also be regarded as lying within Benjamin. Also, Miller's claim that En-rogel cannot be Bir Ayyub because the latter was visible from Davidic Jerusalem (contrasting with the implications of 2 Sam. 17.17) is invalid, since in fact Bir Ayyub is out of sight from the city round a turn in the valley.

90 I am indebted to Prof. J. A. Emerton for reminding me of this point.

91 This fact is noted by R. H. Charles, 'Gehenna' in J. Hastings (ed.), *A Dictionary of the Bible*, vol. 2 (Edinburgh, 1899), p. 119, citing E. Robinson, *Biblical Researches in Palestine*, vol. 1 (London, 1841), pp. 404–5, 3rd edn (1867), p. 274. More recently it has been noted by L. Bailey, 'Gehenna' in *The Interpreter's Dictionary of the Bible Supplementary Volume* (Nashville, 1976), p. 353.

a ready explanation to account for why the fiery sacrifices associated with him in the Hinnom valley developed into the notion of the fires of the hellish Gehenna. There is some comparison here with the Mesopotamian underworld god Nergal, for in Assyrian thought, his cult city Kutu gave its name to the realm of Nergal beneath it.[92]

J. A. Montgomery[93] has shown how natural it was for the valley of Hinnom to become associated with the underworld: Mt. Zion was sometimes equated with the mountain of Paradise (cf. Ps. 46.5 [ET 4]; Isa. 8.6; Ezek. 47.1–12; Joel 4.18 [ET 3.18]; Zech. 14.8 [and later Rev. 21.10ff]; Isa. 11.6–9, 65.25; and note that Gihon is the name of both the paradisiacal river in Gen. 2.13 and the spring in Mt. Zion; also that the mountain of God is equated with Eden in Ezek. 28.12ff). Accordingly, it was only natural for the deep valley below it to be associated with the underworld (cf. Isa. 14.12–15, where Sheol appears to lie at the base of the world mountain). Furthermore, it is worthy of note that a valley closely connected with the Hinnom valley is actually called the valley of Rephaim (Shades), as in Josh. 15.8, 18.16. What Montgomery does not note is the probability that the paradisiacal language associated with Jerusalem was derived from the Jebusites, and that this was therefore probably also the origin of the association of the valley of Hinnom with Sheol and the Molech cult. Ps. 46.5 (ET 4) reads: 'There is a river whose streams make glad the city of God, the holy habitation of the Most High (Elyon).' This paradisiacal river language clearly derives from the Canaanite god El – compare the frequent Ugaritic description of El as dwelling 'at the source of the rivers, amid the springs of the two oceans' (*CTA* 4.IV.21–2, etc.).

It is striking that Ps. 46.5 (ET 4) specifically mentions Elyon, i.e. El-Elyon, the name of the pre-Israelite Jebusite god of Jerusalem, with whom Yahweh was equated, thereby suggesting the Jebusite origin of the paradisiacal language. Moreover, the related Zion Psalm 48 refers to the city in verse 3 (ET 2) as Zaphon, which in Isa. 14.12–13 is likewise associated with Elyon. In Isa. 14.13, Zaphon is the heavenly world mountain and apparently Sheol is represented as lying at its base. Since Zaphon is the heavenly equivalent of Mt. Zion (cf. Ps.

92 Cf. *ANET*, p. 107, 'Descent of Ishtar to the Nether World', line 40. This is noted by Bailey, 'Gehenna', p. 274.

93 'The holy city and Gehenna', *JBL* 27 (1908), 24–47. This article, which offers some interesting arguments tending to support the underworld nature of Molech by virtue of his connection with the valley of Hinnom (Gehenna), is overlooked by Heider, *The Cult of Molek*.

48.3, ET 2), it is natural to suppose that Sheol at its base is likewise equivalent to the valley below Mt. Zion, i.e. the valley of Hinnom.

Since the association of paradisiacal language with Jerusalem is probably Jebusite in origin, it therefore seems plausible to suppose that the connection of the adjacent valley of Hinnom with Sheol is also Jebusite, and consequently that the god Molech was derived by the Israelites from the pre-Israelite inhabitants of Jerusalem. Quite apart from this particular argument, which has never previously been put forward, even by those who have supposed Molech to be Jebusite, the fact that Molech is never mentioned in the Old Testament in association with any place other than the valley of Hinnom, and that the cult is clearly Canaanite, indicates that it may have been appropriated from the local Canaanite inhabitants of Jerusalem, the Jebusites.

Finally, two further texts need to be noted which probably reflect the picture of Molech as an underworld deity.

Job 18.13–14

These verses are part of Bildad's second speech in which he is describing the fate of the wicked: 'By disease his skin is consumed,[94] the first-born of death consumes his limbs. He is torn from the tent in which he trusted, and is brought to the king of terrors.' Death is here personified as 'the king of terrors' (*meleḵ ballāhōṯ*), thus indicating that the underworld could be thought of as being, or having, a king. It is possible that this may be a reminiscence of Molech ('king') if, as is being suggested, he was an underworld deity.

Koran, Sura 43, verse 77

In the Koran, Sura 43, verse 77, Mālik appears as an angel of hell, to whom the damned appeal in order that he intercede with Allah, but Mālik replies that they must remain in hell. Although the text is late, it is possible that this Mālik is also a reminiscence of Molech, the god of the underworld.[95]

94 Reading *yēʾāḵēl biḏᵉway* ʿ*ōrō* 'By disease his skin is consumed' instead of MT *yōʾḵal baddē* ʿ*ōrō* 'It consumes the limbs of his skin', which is meaningless. Moreover, the repetition of 'limbs' in this verse in the MT is not good, and the emendation restores better parallelism with the second half of the verse. Also, it may be noted that reading the passive *yēʾāḵēl* is supported by the LXX and the Peshiṭta. The above emendation was first proposed by G. H. B. Wright, *The Book of Job* (London and Edinburgh, 1883), p. 165, and has been widely accepted.

95 This parallel was previously noted by Jensen, 'Alttestamentlich-Keilschriftliches', p. 237; Tallqvist, *Akkadische Götterepitheta*, p. 359; Healey, '*Malkū*', p. 236, n. 15.

The vocalization of the divine name Molech

Having established that there was a West Semitic god *mlk* who seems to lie behind the Old Testament references to Molech, we must now consider the question whether the vowels are correctly preserved in Molech or whether they have been deliberately distorted in order to echo the Hebrew word *bōšeṯ* 'shame'.

The latter view was first put forward by A. Geiger[96] and has been widely accepted since his day. It rests on the fact that there is evidence that the name of the god Baal was sometimes replaced by the word *bōšeṯ* 'shame' in the Hebrew text[97] and that the name of the goddess Astarte (surely originally Ashtart in Hebrew) has become Ashtoreth in the Old Testament. Since the divine name Molech (cf. Topheth) also has these vowels, it is attractive to suppose that the vocalization of this divine name has likewise been distorted, which thereby meant that this detested deity no longer had to be referred to by the elevated word *meleḵ* 'king' (cf. *baʿal* 'lord').

This generally accepted series of views has been questioned by M. Tsevat,[98] but his arguments are unconvincing. Briefly, his arguments may be summarized as follows. With regard to Ashtoreth, he claims that we have no means of knowing that Ashtart was the original Hebrew vocalization. As for *bōšeṯ*, he believes that this does not mean 'shame' when it occurs in personal names (e.g. Ish-bosheth in 2 Sam. 2.10, etc., cf. Eshbaal, 1 Chron. 8.33, 9.39) but is rather cognate with Akkadian *bāštu* 'dignity, pride, vigour', and functions as a divine name or epithet. He thinks it militates against the generally held view that in 2 Sam. 11.21 we read not of Jerubbosheth but of Jerubbesheth (Jerubbaal/Gideon, Judg. 6.32) in the MT, and finds it curious that the name Meribaal (or Meribbaal, 1 Chron. 8.34, 9.40) should have been distorted to Mephibosheth (2 Sam. 4.4, 9.6, 19.25, etc.; there is another Mephibosheth in 2 Sam. 21.8). Rather than the element *baʿal* having been distorted to *bōšeṯ* in these names, he believes that these are cases where individuals bore two names. Since he claims that

96 *Urschrift und Uebersetzungen der Bibel* (Breslau, 1857), p. 301.

97 This was first argued by O. Thenius, *Die Bücher Samuels* (Leipzig, 1842), pp. 142, 175. Cf. too A. Geiger, 'Der Baal in den hebräischen Eigennamen', *ZDMG* 16 (1862), 728–32.

98 'Ishbosheth and congeners: the names and their study', *HUCA* 46 (1975), 71–87. That the name Molech was influenced by the vowels of the word *bōšeṯ* was earlier questioned by K. Dronkert, *De Molochdienst in het Oude Testament* (Leiden, 1953), pp. 12–21, but his arguments are likewise uncompelling. Cf. too Heider, *The Cult of Molek*, pp. 223–8 (on which see below).

there is no evidence for *bōšeṯ* as a defamation of *baʿal* or for the view that the vowels of the name of Astarte have been distorted to Ashtoreth, he argues that it is preferable to suppose that the god's name actually was Molech.

As I have already said, Tsevat's arguments are unconvincing. As for Ashtoreth, all the evidence points to an original vocalization Ashtart when we consider that all the relevant parallels have an *a* in the second syllable, not only Greek Astarte, Egyptian ʿA-ś-tá-r-tu, and Akkadian Ishtar, but also the Arabian name for the male deity Athtar. As for *bošeṯ*, to connect this with Akkadian *bāštu* would involve creating a hitherto unattested Hebrew word without adequate supporting evidence. Tsevat fails to explain why, in his view, it is precisely certain individuals with the element *baʿal* in their name who also have a name including the element *bōšeṯ*, and no others.[99] There are also a few passages in the prophets where the word *bōšeṯ* refers to the god Baal and these are, curiously, unmentioned by Tsevat. Compare Hos. 9.10, 'But they came to Baal-peor, and consecrated themselves to the shameful thing (*bōšeṯ*), and became detestable like the thing they loved', and Jer. 11.13, 'For your gods have become as many as your cities, O Judah; and as many as the streets of Jerusalem are the altars you have set up to the shameful thing (*bōšeṯ*), altars to burn incense to Baal'. Mention may also be made of Jer. 3.24, where reference to Baal is surely intended, although not explicitly mentioned: 'But from our youth the shameful thing (*bōšeṯ*) has devoured all for which our fathers laboured, their flocks and their herds, their sons and their daughters.' Now since these passages have a condemnatory tone, the meaning 'shameful thing' seems more appropriate than 'dignity, pride, vigour' for *bōšeṯ*; this is clearly the case in Hos. 9.10, where after the reference to *bōšeṯ* we read that the Baal worshippers 'became detestable (*šiqqūṣīm*) like the thing they loved'. *Bōšeṯ* must therefore also mean 'shameful thing' in the personal names mentioned above. The fact that 2 Sam. 11.21 refers to Jerubbesheth rather than Jerubbosheth is no problem, since the latter must have been what was originally intended in view of the parallels, a point overlooked by the Massoretes in their vocalization in this instance. Again, there is no problem in Meribaal (or Meribbaal) having been distorted not merely to Meribosheth but to Mephibosheth.

99 After I had written this, Prof. D. Pardee kindly informed me that he had previously noted the point against Tsevat made in this sentence in 'Letters from Tel Arad', *UF* 10 (1978), 314, n. 106.

There are grounds for believing, therefore, that the word *bōšeṯ* could substitute for the divine name Baal and that the vowels of this word were used to distort the name of the goddess Astarte. When we find another detested deity, Molech, with the same vowels it is therefore attractive to suppose that the same cause has been operative. We should in any case most naturally expect the true name of the deity in Hebrew to have been *meleḵ* or conceivably *mōlēḵ* (the participial form), and the fact that the name would literally mean 'king', a noble epithet, makes it easy to see how it could be subject to distortion (cf. Baal, lit. 'lord'). Heider's view[100] that Hebrew *mōleḵ* is itself a participial form is clearly forced, since we should naturally expect the word to be vocalized *mōlēḵ*, not *mōleḵ*, with the emphasis on the final, not the penultimate syllable, if this were the case. Heider seems to be driven to this view because he wrongly supposes that there are no other examples of the distortion of divine names with the vowels of *bōšeṯ*. As we have seen, however, this is clearly the case with the name of the goddess Ashtoreth, distorted from Ashtart (Astarte).

The covenant with Death in Isaiah 28.15, 18: an allusion to the Molech cult

In the light of the evidence presented above that Molech was an underworld deity, I now propose to identify a further allusion to the Molech cult which has hitherto remained undetected. This occurs in Isa. 28.15, 18, where the prophet speaks of the rulers in Jerusalem making a covenant or agreement with Death and Sheol, with the avowed intention of averting national disaster, which is clearly a reference to a potential Assyrian invasion of Judah. Isaiah, however, regards this ploy as quite futile. It would be as well first to cite the verses in context.

Isaiah 28.14–22

14 Therefore hear the word of the Lord, you scoffers,
who rule this people in Jerusalem!
15 Because you have said, 'We have made a covenant with Death,
and we have made an agreement with Sheol.

100 Heider, *The Cult of Molek*, pp. 223–8.

When the overwheming scourge[101] passes through,[102] it will not come to
us,
for we have made lies our refuge, and we have taken shelter in falsehood' –
16 Therefore thus says the Lord God, 'Behold I am laying[103] a stone in Zion,
a tested stone,[104]
a precious cornerstone, of a sure foundation; he who believes will not be
perturbed.[105]

101 Reading *šōṭ* for *šīṭ* with *qere* and 1QIsa^{a}, thus agreeing with the parallel passage in v. 18. J. Barth, ' שוט שטף ', *ZAW* 33 (1913), 306–7 (cf. S. Poznański, 'Zu שוט שטף ', *ZAW* 36 (1916), 119–20), was unhappy with the allusion to 'scourge' in this context and proposed the rendering 'flood', and this has been widely followed. This view is, however, to be rejected. It is true that the root *šṭp*, here applied to the *šōṭ*, is primarily used in connection with water and that v. 17 applies storm imagery to the Assyrians. However, this does not warrant the translation of *šōṭ* by 'flood', thereby creating a *hapax legomenon* (J. Barth's finding of the meaning 'flood' also in Job 9.23 being unconvincing, 'Zu שוט "Flut"', *ZAW* 34 [1914], 69). There is a certain similarity between the expressions *šōṭ* 'scourge' and *maṭṭeh* and *šēḇeṭ* 'rod' (cf. the evident interchange between them in Isa. 10.24, 26), the latter expressions being employed of the Assyrians in Isa. 10.5 as *šōṭ* is in Isa. 28.15, 18. It is significant that, in Isa. 30.31 and 32, the expressions *šēḇeṭ* and *maṭṭeh* are closely associated with the destructive storm imagery of Isa. 30.30, which is similar to that of Isa. 28.17 (cf. 28.2). This suggests that it is entirely natural for *šōṭ* 'scourge' to be employed in a similar way and unnecessary to render it as 'flood'. H. Gese, 'Die strömende Geisel des Hadad und Jesaja 28, 15 und 18' in A. Kuschke and E. Kutsch (eds.), *Archäologie und Altes Testament* (Festschrift für Kurt Galling, Tübingen, 1970), pp. 127–34, has argued that the *šōṭ* 'whip' in Isa. 28.15, 18 representing Assyria is taken over from the symbolism of the god Hadad, who is sometimes depicted holding a whip, which denotes the lightning. However, it seems to me unnecessary for Hadad symbolism to be imported into the text. In Isa. 28 Assyria is surely conceived as the agent of *Yahweh's* judgment, and it would therefore seem inappropriate for the symbolism of some other god to be brought in at this point. Further, in spite of the one reference which Gese cites where Shalmaneser III speaks of himself as 'descending upon them like Adad when he makes a rainstorm pour down', it is overwhelmingly to the god Ashur, not Adad, that the Assyrian kings attributed their victories. This, therefore, makes it improbable that symbolism from the god Adad would be applied to an Assyrian king in Isa. 28.

102 Reading *ya‘ᵃḇōr* with the *qere*, rather than *kethibh* *‘āḇar*. Cf. v. 18.

103 Reading *yōsēḏ* for MT *yissaḏ*, with 1QIsa^{b}, Aquila, Symmachus, Theodotion, Peshiṭta and Targum, as the 3rd person sing. perf. form *yissaḏ* is clearly inappropriate after *hinᵉnī* 'Behold *I*'.

104 The expression *’eḇen bōḥan*, here rendered 'tested stone', is a noteworthy crux. It has sometimes been taken as an Egyptian loan-word *bḫn-w* 'diorite, granite', but it seems simpler to take it as the *pu‘al* participle of the verb *bḥn* 'to test' (cf. Ezek. 21.18). Since it is clear from the context that the stone is of firm foundation and is a symbol of confidence, the meaning 'tested stone' is appropriate. On the theological interpretation of the stone in Isa. 28.16 see, in addition to the commentaries, J. Lindblom, 'Der Eckstein in Jes. 28, 16' in *Interpretationes ad Vetus Testamentum pertinentes Sigmundo Mowinckel septuagenario missae* (Oslo, 1955), pp. 123–32.

105 The normal meaning of *ḥūš* is 'to hasten', but the translation 'he who believes will

17 And I will make justice the measuring line and righteousness the levelling instrument;
and hail will sweep away the refuge of lies, and waters will overwhelm the shelter.'
18 Then your covenant with Death will be annulled, and your agreement with Sheol will not stand;
when the overwhelming scourge passes through, you will be beaten down by it.
19 As often as it passes through it will take you;
for morning by morning it will pass through, by day and by night;
and it will be nothing but terror to understand the message.
20 For the bed is too short to stretch oneself on it, and the covering too narrow to wrap oneself in it.
21 For the Lord will rise up as on Mount Perazim,
he will be enraged as in the valley of Gibeon;
to do his deed – strange is his deed! And to do his work – alien is his work.
22 Now, do not scoff, lest your bonds be made strong;
for I have heard destruction decreed
by the Lord God of hosts upon the whole land.

Commentators disagree when it comes to the question of the interpretation of the covenant or agreement with Death and Sheol in verses 15 and 18. The most popular view seems to be that it is a veiled allusion to a political alliance with Egypt against Assyria in the time of Hezekiah[106] (cf. Isa. 18, 20, 30.1–7, 31.1–3), but there is disagreement when the attempt is made to explain why Egypt should be referred to in this obscure and enigmatic fashion, which is nowhere else attested. Sometimes it has been held that Death and Sheol are employed to represent Egypt because of the religious preoccupation of Egypt with death[107] or with the cult of Osiris,[108] the underworld deity, but this seems fanciful. Others have held that Death and Sheol are mentioned because Osiris would have been a witness to the treaty

not hasten' does not yield good sense. Clearly it means 'he who believes will not be perturbed', and this is supported by the evidence of Akkadian *ḫāšu* 'to worry', Arabic *ḥāsa(w)* I and VIII 'to be perplexed, bewildered', and Ethiopic *taḥaw(w)asa* 'to be moved, shaken', as well as by the renderings in the Peshiṭta 'he shall fear' and Targum 'they shall be shaken'. Cf. G. R. Driver, 'Studies in the vocabulary of the Old Testament. II', *JTS* 32 (1931), 253–5; F. Ellermeier, 'Das Verbum חוש in Koh 2 25', *ZAW* 75, NS 34 (1963), 197–217.

106 W. R. Smith, *The Prophets of Israel*, 2nd edn (London, 1919), p. 284, thought rather of an alliance with Assyria, but no scholar today follows this view. The same objections apply as to the view that Death and Sheol symbolize Egypt. Cf. below. 107 A. Schoors, *Jesaja* (Roermond, 1972), p. 167.

108 R. E. Clements, *Isaiah 1–39* (London, 1980), p. 229.

between Egypt and Judah,[109] but against this view it may be noted that the language used (see Isa. 28.15, 18) implies that Death or Sheol was the covenant *partner* and not simply a witness. Other fanciful views are that the allusion to the covenant with Death is a figurative way of saying that the rulers were 'dead certain' of their safety because of their alliance with Egypt,[110] or that they were acting as though they were immortal in the face of their imminent danger because of their alliance.[111] Recently, it has been suggested that Egypt is here being symbolized by rites such as those of the Molech cult,[112] but it is surely odd that Egypt should be represented in this way by a Canaanite rite. A final view associating the imagery with Egypt holds that it is employed because Egypt is a deadly power which swallows up all who go down to her.[113] However, this no more than the preceding suggestions carries conviction, since not only is it odd that Egypt should fail to be mentioned by name if it were being alluded to, but it is also significant that the covenant partner is spoken of as 'lies' (*kāzāḇ*) and 'falsehood' (*šeqer*), terms frequently employed elsewhere in the Old Testament of pagan deities (cf. Isa. 44.20, 57.4; Jer. 3.23, 10.14 [=51.17], 13.25, 16.19; Hab. 2.18 (*šeqer*); Amos 2.4 (*kāzāb*), also note Isa. 57.11 [*piʿel* of √*kzb*]).

Rather than seeing an allusion to a covenant with Egypt, it is therefore more natural and straightforward to suppose that it is a question of an agreement with an underworld deity. Some, admittedly, have thought in terms of necromancy,[114] i.e. consultation of the spirits of the dead, and this might be thought to be consistent with the reference to 'lies' and 'falsehood', since dead spirits are occasionally spoken of as 'gods' (cf. 1 Sam. 28.13; Isa. 8.19), but over against this it should be noted that Isa. 28.15, 18 do not speak of 'the dead' in the

109 H. Schmidt, *Die grossen Propheten*, 2nd edn (Göttingen, 1924), p. 93; O. Procksch, *Jesaia*, vol. 1 (Leipzig, 1930), p. 360 (possibly); G. Fohrer, *Das Buch Jesaja*, vol. 1 (Zurich and Stuttgart, 1962), p. 57.

110 F. Huber, *Jahwe, Juda und die anderen Völker beim Propheten Jesaja* (*BZAW* 137, 1976), p. 96.

111 O. Kaiser, *Der Prophet Jesaja Kapitel 13–39* (Göttingen, 1973), p. 200 (ET, *Isaiah 13–39* [London, 1974], pp. 251–2).

112 H. Wildberger, *Jesaja*, vol. 3 (Neukirchen-Vluyn, 1982), pp. 1073–5.

113 M. A. Klopfenstein, *Die Lüge nach dem Alten Testament* (Zurich and Frankfurt, 1964), p. 150.

114 G. W. Wade, *The Book of the Prophet Isaiah* (London, 1911), p. 180; J. Skinner, *Isaiah I–XXXIX* (Cambridge, 1915), p. 225; E. König, *Das Buch Jesaja* (Gütersloh, 1926), pp. 253–4; E. Power, 'Isaias (Isaiah)' in B. Orchard, E. F. Sutcliffe, R. C. Fuller, R. Russell (eds.), *A Catholic Commentary on Holy Scripture* (London, 1953), p. 558.

plural (*mēṯīm*), which we should expect if this were the case (cf. Isa. 8.19), but rather in the singular of Death and Sheol. Also it may be argued that consultation is not the same as a covenant.[115] By a process of elimination, therefore, we are driven to the conclusion that the rulers of Jerusalem are being accused of concluding a pact with an underworld deity in order to avert national disaster. Which particular underworld deity is in mind? The view that it is the Egyptian god Osiris, a suggestion sometimes made without any assumption of a treaty with Egypt,[116] is open to the objection that it is difficult to believe that the rulers in Jerusalem would have placed their confidence in this particular foreign deity. More frequently scholars have thought of the Canaanite underworld god Mot,[117] sometimes even going as far as to translate *māweṯ* in Isa. 28.15, 18 as Mot rather than Death. This is an attractive suggestion, but hitherto commentators have been unable to produce supporting evidence that a Canaanite underworld god cult was practised in Judah at this time with the purpose of averting the Assyrian threat.

Surprisingly, scholars have overlooked the Molech cult.[118] It is the present writer's contention that it is this to which the allusions to the covenant or agreement with Death and Sheol in Isa. 28.15, 18 refer. As we have seen above, Molech was indeed a Canaanite underworld deity. Furthermore, it was precisely during the period of the Assyrian hegemony that his cult particularly flourished, as the offering up of their children by Ahaz and Manasseh testifies (cf. 2 Kgs. 16.3, 21.6). These specific examples show that the Molech cult had a following in the ruling class, the same group as is associated with the covenant with Death in Isa. 28. Moreover, there can surely be no doubt that the reason for the sudden revival of the Molech cult in this period, along with other Canaanite syncretistic practices, was as a response to the Assyrian threat. Desperate circumstances required desperate measures (cf. Mesha's sacrifice in 2 Kgs. 3.27 and Carthaginian

115 For the point made in this sentence, I am indebted to the Revd. B. A. Mastin.

116 B. Duhm, *Das Buch Jesaia*, 4th edn (Göttingen, 1922), p. 200.

117 R. B. Y. Scott, 'The book of Isaiah: chapters 1–39. Introduction and exegesis' in *Interpreter's Bible*, vol. 5 (New York and Nashville, 1956), p. 317 ('Perhaps . . . Mot . . . or . . . Osiris'); G. R. Driver, '"Another little drink" – Isaiah 28:1–22' in P. R. Ackroyd and B. Lindars (eds.), *Words and Meanings. Essays Presented to David Winton Thomas* (Cambridge, 1968), pp. 57–8, who thinks the vowels of *mwt* in MT may be wrong; A. S. Herbert, *The Book of the Prophet Isaiah* (Cambridge, 1973), p. 164; W. H. Irwin, *Isaiah 28–33. Translation with Philological Notes* (Rome, 1977), p. 26.

118 It is true that Wildberger, *Jesaja*, vol. 3, p. 1075, saw an allusion to the Molech cult but for him this was simply a symbol for Egypt, as I have noted above.

human sacrifice in time of need) and the offering of human sacrifice was thought to possess especially strong apotropaic power.

Although there is no explicit statement that the Molech cult was thought of in covenantal terms (cf. Isa. 28.15, 18), the *do ut des* concept underlying the offering of children to Molech might easily have lent itself to expression in such terms. Moreover, it is interesting to note the striking parallel between Isa. 28.15, 18, with their allusion to the making of a covenant or agreement with Death and Sheol, and Isa. 57.9, which says of the Molech worshippers, 'You journeyed to Molech[119] with oil and multiplied your unguents, you sent your envoys far off, and sent down even to Sheol'. The language employed here is certainly suggestive of the making of an agreement with Molech/Sheol, and it is worthy of note that the word rendered 'envoys' (*ṣîrîm*) is actually used in Isa. 18.2 of those engaged in forging a political alliance or covenant. It may also be noted that there are other parallels between the passages in Isa. 28 and 57, thus further tending to support their correlation. In Isa. 57.11, the verse immediately following the allusion to the Molech cult in verses 9–10, and therefore most naturally referring to it, Yahweh declares, 'Whom did you dread and fear, so that you lied (*ṯᵉḵazzēḇî*), and did not remember me, did not give me a thought?' This recalls Isa. 28.15, 17, where, as we have noted earlier, the covenant with Death is spoken of as involving taking refuge in 'lies' (*ḵāzāḇ*). The use of the word 'refuge' (*maḥseh*) in Isa. 28.15 in relation to the covenant with Death also seems to find an echo in Isa. 57, for in verse 13 Yahweh declares, 'When you cry out, let your collection of idols deliver you! The wind will carry them all off, a breath will take them away. But he who takes refuge (*wᵉhaḥōseh*) in me shall possess the land, and shall inherit my holy mountain'. The clear implication of this is that the people were taking refuge in the idolatry mentioned in the previous verses, including the Molech cult.

In the light of the above considerations it may be concluded that there is good reason to believe that Isa. 28.15, 18 allude to the Molech cult. This conclusion has ramifications for the probable date of the section of which these verses form a part: Isa. 28.14–22. The majority of commentators date this passage to the time of Hezekiah, usually in the period 705–1 B.C., a conclusion seemingly supported by the common view that the covenant with Death of Isa. 28.15, 18 refers to the anti-Assyrian Egyptian alliance of that time. As the above

119 See above, pp. 50–2.

discussion has shown, however, this interpretation of the covenant with Death is to be rejected, the result being that the grounds commonly alleged for a dating in the reign of Hezekiah no longer hold. On the contrary, the conclusion that Isa. 28.15, 18 allude to the Molech cult rather inclines one to move away from a date in the time of Hezekiah and towards an earlier one in the reign of Ahaz.[120] Both Ahaz and Manasseh are mentioned as having offered up one of their children (to Molech, cf. 2 Kgs. 16.3, 21.6), whereas Hezekiah is reported to have undertaken a radical purge of syncretistic cults (cf. 2 Kgs. 18.3–6). Since, according to the superscription to the book of Isaiah (Isa. 1.1), this prophet's preaching did not extend beyond the reign of Hezekiah, and since there are no grounds for believing the section Isa. 28.14–22 to be a later addition to the authentic words of Isaiah, we may exclude the reign of Manasseh as a possible time of composition of these verses and fasten on the reign of Ahaz as their likely period of origin. This conclusion is consistent with the fact that Isa. 28:14–22 is appended to, and bears a number of striking literary parallels to, Isa. 28:1–13, verses proclaiming the downfall of the Northern Kingdom, and therefore dating to the period before 722 B.C. and most likely to the reign of Ahaz. The striking literary parallels between the two sections are as follows: with verse 2, 'like a storm of hail (*bārāḏ*), a destroying tempest, like a storm of mighty, overwhelming waters (*mayim . . . šōṭᵉp̱īm*)', compare verse 17, 'and hail (*ḇārāḏ*) will sweep away the refuge of lies, and waters will overwhelm (*mayim yišṭōp̱ū*) the shelter', and also verses 15, 18, 'the overwhelming (*šōṭēp̱*) scourge', and with verse 9, 'will he explain the message' (*yāḇīn šᵉmūʿāh*), compare verse 19, 'to understand the message (*hāḇīn šᵉmūʿāh*)'.

In conclusion, then, it may be argued that the covenant with Death in Isa. 28.15, 18 alludes neither to an Egyptian alliance, necromancy, nor simply to Mot, but specifically to the cult of the underworld god Molech. The passage probably derives from the time of Ahaz, when the Assyrian threat encouraged the revival of this apotropaic ritual as a desperate measure to stave off national catastrophe.

120 A few scholars, deviating from the majority view, have also dated this passage before 722 B.C. and therefore ascribed it to the reign of Ahaz or even earlier. Cf. A. Bentzen, *Jesaja*, vol. 1 (Copenhagen, 1944), p. 216; Lindblom, 'Der Eckstein in Jes. 28, 16' in *Interpretationes ad Vetus Testamentum*, pp. 128f; R. Fey, *Amos und Jesaja* (*WMANT* 12, Neukirchen-Vluyn, 1963), p. 122.

Molech, Yahweh and the offering of the first-born

Many scholars have concluded that, although Molech may have been a foreign god in origin, those who worshipped him equated him with Yahweh.[121] Furthermore, it is sometimes supposed that the human sacrifice offered to Molech is to be identified with the offering of the first-born to Yahweh mentioned in the Pentateuch.[122] The equation with Yahweh has been suggested especially by the threefold repetition in the prose sections of Jeremiah that Yahweh had not commanded the Molech sacrifices, which could imply that there were those who thought he had. Thus, Jer. 32.35 declares: 'They built the high places of Baal in the valley of the son of Hinnom, to offer up their sons and daughters to Molech, though I did not command them, nor did it enter into my mind, that they should do this abomination, to cause Judah to sin.' Further, although Molech is not explicitly mentioned, the reference to the valley of Hinnom, well attested as the seat of the Molech cult, as well as the close verbal parallelism generally with Jer. 32.35, leaves no doubt that it is the Molech cult which is being referred to in Jer. 7.31 and 19.5. The former passage reads, 'And they have built the high place[123] of Topheth, which is in the valley of Hinnom, to burn their sons and daughters in the fire; which I did not command, nor did it come into my mind', and the latter passage declares, 'and (they) have built the high places of Baal to burn their sons in the fire,[124] which I did not command or decree, nor did it come into my mind'.

The implication drawn by some that these verses from Jeremiah suggest that the Molech worshippers thought that Yahweh had commanded the sacrifices has led to the view that the command is that concerning the offering of the first-born in the Pentateuch. In its unqualified form this occurs in Exod. 22.28f (ET 29f): 'The first-born of your sons you shall give me. You shall do likewise with your oxen and your sheep; seven days it shall be with its dam; on the eighth day

121 Those equating Molech with Yahweh include W. Eichrodt, *Theologie des Alten Testaments*, vol. 1, 5th edn (Leipzig, 1957–65), pp. 89f, 123 (ET, *Theology of the Old Testament*, vol. 1 [London, 1967], pp. 149f, 197); M. Buber, *Königtum Gottes*, 3rd edn (Heidelberg, 1956), p. 173 (ET, *Kingship of God*, 3rd edn [London, 1967], p. 180); H. Irsigler, *Gottesgericht und Jahwetag* (St Ottilien, 1977), p. 34.

122 E.g. Eissfeldt, *Molk als Opferbegriff*, pp. 48–56; I. D. Miller, 'Other gods and idols in the period of Hosea' (Unpublished M.Litt. thesis, Cambridge University, 1975), pp. 63f.

123 Cf. above, p. 17, n. 4.

124 Omitting *ʿōlōṯ labbāʿal* 'as burnt offerings to Baal' with the LXX. Cf. above, p. 17, n. 5.

you shall give it to me.' We find the same law in Exod. 34.19f, generally ascribed to the J source, and in Exod. 13.2, 12f, 15, from the P source, except that in these passages a modification is made to the original law and provision is made for the redemption of the first-born. Thus, Exod. 34.19f declares: 'All that opens the womb is mine, all your male cattle, the firstlings of cow and sheep. The firstlings of an ass you shall redeem with a lamb, or if you will not redeem it you shall break its neck. All the first-born of your sons you shall redeem. And none shall appear before me empty.' And in Exod. 13.2, 12f, 15, we read:

> Consecrate to me all the first-born; whatever is the first to open the womb among the people of Israel, both of man and of beast, is mine . . . you shall devote to the Lord all that first opens the womb. All the firstlings of your cattle that are males shall be the Lord's. Every firstling of an ass you shall redeem with a lamb, or if you will not redeem it you shall break its neck. Every first-born of man among your sons you shall redeem . . . For when Pharaoh stubbornly refused to let us go, the Lord slew all the first-born in the land of Egypt, both the first-born of man and the first-born of cattle. Therefore I sacrifice to the Lord all the males that first open the womb; but all the first-born of my sons I redeem.

It is interesting to note that the verb *hʿbyr* 'to devote' used in verse 12 is the same as that employed in connection with the Molech cult.

What might further seem to suggest a connection between the Molech cult and the offering of the first-born is the fact that the references to the latter outside the Pentateuch date from the period when we know that the Molech cult was flourishing. Thus Mic. 6.7, whether deriving from the prophet himself or, as is usually thought, from a later redactor, raises the question, 'Shall I give my first-born for my transgression, the fruit of my body for the sin of my soul?' The question seems to be raised in all seriousness, even though the option is finally rejected. However, the prophet Ezekiel, in a remarkable passage (Ezek. 20.25f), has Yahweh declare: 'Moreover, I gave them statutes that were not good and ordinances by which they could not have life; and I defiled them through their very gifts in making them offer all their first-born, that I might horrify them; I did it that they might know that I am the Lord.' It has sometimes been supposed[125] that in this last passage Ezekiel is claiming those human sacrifices to be of divine origin which are expressly denied to be such in the passages quoted earlier from Jeremiah (Jer. 7.31, 19.5, 32.35).

125 E.g. Miller, 'Other gods and idols', pp. 63f.

What are we to say of all this? Is it the case that Yahweh was equated with Molech and that the Molech sacrifices were the first-born offered to Yahweh? I shall deal with the second point first. Here I agree with H. Gese and G. C. Heider,[126] who have recently argued that the Molech sacrifices and the offering of the first-born cannot be equated. Thus, first, whereas the latter specifically concern the first-born and no others (cf. Exod. 13.2, 12–15, 22.28f, ET 29f, 34.19f; Ezek. 20.25f; Mic. 6.7) and make no mention of Molech, the passages referring to Molech never refer to the first-born but speak rather of the offering of children generally. A second significant difference is that the law of the first-born involves only the sons (Exod. 13.12–15, 22.28f, ET 29f, 34.19f; Num. 3.12f, 40ff, 8.16–18; cf. Deut. 15.19f), whereas the references to the Molech cult repeatedly mention the offering of daughters as well as sons (cf. Deut. 12.31, 18.10; Jer. 3.24, 7.31, 32.35; Ezek. 16.20; 2 Kgs. 17.17, 23.10; Ps. 106.37f). Even Ezekiel, who accepts that Yahweh had demanded the offering of the first-born (Ezek. 20.25f), cannot have been referring to the Molech cult, since elsewhere he strongly opposes child sacrifices (including daughters) devoted to idols (Ezek. 16.20f, 20.31, 23.37–9),[127] which surely included the Molech cult. It is clear therefore that the Molech sacrifices are not to be equated with the first-born offered to Yahweh.

May it not still be the case, however, that Molech was equated with Yahweh in the eyes of his worshippers? This too I am inclined to reject. It seems inherently improbable that Yahweh should be identified with an underworld god, which is what Molech was, as we have seen. For long periods the underworld was a realm without close associations with Yahweh (cf. Pss. 6.6, ET 5, 88.11–13, ET 10–12),

126 H. Gese, 'Ezechiel 20, 25f. und die Erstgeburtsopfer' in H. Donner, R. Hanhart and R. Smend (eds.), *Beiträge zur Alttestamentlichen Theologie* (Festschrift für Walther Zimmerli zum 70. Geburtstag, Göttingen, 1977), pp. 143–5; G. C. Heider, *The Cult of Molek*, p. 254. Heider does not seem to be aware of Gese's study.

127 It should be noted that the references to child sacrifice in Ezek. 20.31 and 23.37–9 are redactional according to W. Zimmerli in his Ezekiel commentary. Even if this is correct, we are still left with authentic Ezekielian material in the other two passages, one of which speaks of the offering of sons and daughters to idols and the other of the offering of the first-born (i.e. of sons) to Yahweh. It is true that O. Kaiser, 'Den Erstgeborenen deiner Söhne sollst du mir geben' in O. Kaiser (ed.), *Denkender Glaube. Festschrift Carl Heinz Ratschow* (Berlin and New York, 1976), p. 40, n. 57, regards all the Ezekielian allusions to child sacrifices as later insertions. He also rejects the historicity of the various allusions to the Molech cult in the Deuteronomistic history, which he sees as modelled on the reference to child sacrifice in Deut. 18.10 (itself held to be redactional), and the allusions in Leviticus he claims are late. Whilst Kaiser's article is remarkable for its bibliographical thoroughness, his conclusions seem unjustifiably radical.

and, since in certain syncretistic circles Yahweh was equated with Baal (cf. Hos. 2.18, ET 16), it would be surprising for him to be equated at the same time with the opposing power of the underworld. Moreover, it should be noted that the Molech cult did not take place in Yahweh's temple in Jerusalem but in a separate site in the Hinnom valley. This suggests that we have to do with separate deities. Further, the verses in Jer. 7.31, 19.5 and 32.35 which have often been thought to lend support to the equation of Molech with Yahweh do not in fact do so. There Yahweh declares with respect to the Molech sacrifices, 'I did not command, nor did it come into my mind'. The point has already been made above that if some people thought that Yahweh had commanded these sacrifices, this was certainly not on the basis of any command in the Pentateuch, since the law of the first-born was quite different. There is, however, an important point which has generally been overlooked, though it was noted by A. Kuenen[128] in the nineteenth century. This is the fact that the expression 'I did not command' found in these Deuteronomistic prose passages in Jeremiah is also found in the related Deuteronomic literature in Deut. 17.3 in a similar context of idolatry. There the spectre is raised of one who 'has gone and served other gods and worshipped them, or the sun or the moon or any of the host of heaven, *which I have not commanded*'. Clearly there can be no question here of people having equated Yahweh with the other gods, sun or moon or host of heaven, and there is therefore no more reason why Yahweh should have been thought identical with Molech when the same language is used in Jeremiah. Most translations now, in fact, render *ʾašer lōʾ ṣiwwīṯī* as 'which I forbade' in Deut. 17.3, rather than as 'which I did not command'. This would suit the Molech passages in Jer. 7.31, 19.5 and 32.35, since Deuteronomy does in fact forbid human sacrifice (cf. Deut. 12.31, 18.10). However, it might be the case that the repeated phrase 'nor did it come into my mind' (Jer. 7.31, 19.5, 32.35) does indicate that it is not simply a case of Yahweh forbidding Molech sacrifices, but that there is here a protest against the notion that Yahweh himself has given consent to them. But this does not mean that Yahweh and Molech were equated.

It would seem, therefore, that there are no grounds for equating Molech with Yahweh. On the other hand, it is clear that those who engaged in the Molech cult did not see themselves as faithless to

128 'Critische bijdragen tot de geschiedenis van den Israëlietischen godsdienst. III. Jahveh en Moloch', *Theologisch Tijdschrift*, 2 (1868), 585.

Yahweh, in spite of the protests found in the Old Testament. Thus, Ezek. 23.38–9 declares: 'Moreover this they have done to me: they have defiled my sanctuary on the same day and profaned my sabbaths. For when they had slaughtered their children in sacrifice to their idols, on the same day they came into my sanctuary to profane it.' Similar language is used in Lev. 20.3, which alludes to the man who 'has given one of his children to Molech, defiling my sanctuary and profaning my holy name'. Again, in Zeph. 1.5, the prophet refers to 'those who bow down and swear to the Lord and yet swear by their King (*malkām*)'. Some scholars[129] emend 'their King' (*malkām*) to Milcom (*milkōm*; cf. the Lucianic recension of the LXX, the Vulgate and the Peshiṭta), but it seems on balance preferable to retain the MT and understand it as referring to Molech,[130] since there is considerable evidence of the attraction of his cult to Israelites, including Yahweh worshippers, at this time,[131] which cannot be said of Milcom, whose cult was introduced by Solomon as a diplomatic measure for his Ammonite wives. Whatever one may conclude about Zeph. 1.5, it is clear from the above references that there were Israelites who worshipped both Molech and Yahweh, though, as we have seen, they were not equated. This is of a piece with the general syncretism of the time, for we know that Baal, Asherah and the host of heaven were worshipped in the very temple of Yahweh in the time of Manasseh (2 Kgs. 21.3), which indicates that they were regarded as part of Yahweh's pantheon. Although Molech was not actually worshipped in the temple, his cult was not felt incompatible with that of Yahweh on the part of those who offered him human sacrifice.

There are a number of other passages in the Old Testament where Yahweh is associated in one way or another with human sacrifice, namely Abraham's near offering of Isaac in Gen. 22.1–14 and the incident of Jephthah's daughter in Judg. 11.30–40. It has also been suggested that the affair of David's executing seven of Saul's

129 Those reading Milcom include A. van Hoonacker, *Les Douze Petits Prophètes* (Paris, 1908), p. 510; E. Sellin, *Das Zwölfprophetenbuch*, 2nd and 3rd edns (Leipzig, 1929–30), p. 420; F. Horst in T. H. Robinson and F. Horst, *Die zwölf kleinen Propheten*, 2nd edn (Tübingen, 1954), p. 190.

130 So G. F. Moore, 'Milcom' in *Encyclopaedia Biblica*, vol. 3 (London, 1902), col. 3085; Gray, *The Legacy of Canaan*, p. 172. Others retain MT *malkām* but see a reference to some other god than Molech, e.g. Baal. Cf. Sabottka, *Zephanja*, pp. 24f, and A. S. Kapelrud, *The Message of the Prophet Zephaniah* (Oslo, Bergen and Tromsø, 1975), pp. 23f.

131 Interestingly the Molech cult, implied in 2 Kgs. 21.6 (cf. 23.10), follows references to the worship of Baal and the host of heaven in 2 Kgs. 21.3, 5, which is comparable to the situation in Zeph. 1.4f.

descendants to appease the Gibeonites in 2 Sam. 21.1–14 may reflect a fertility ritual of human sacrifice.[132] The first of these passages (Gen. 22.1–14) has been related to the Molech cult by F. Stolz,[133] and therefore calls for further discussion. Over against the view of most scholars, Stolz believes that the mountain in the land of Moriah in Gen. 22.2 is to be equated with Jerusalem, in accordance with 2 Chron. 3.1, where Mt. Moriah is identified with the Temple Mount on Zion. He further thinks this view is supported by the fact that it was specifically in Jerusalem that human sacrifice became a problem. He sees the sacrifices of Ahaz and Manasseh (2 Kgs. 16.3, 21.6) as relating to the cult of Molech-Shalem, the Jebusite god of Jerusalem with whom Yahweh was equated, and he believes that Gen. 22 is directed against the human sacrifice involved in this cult: behind *yahweh yir'eh* (Gen. 22.14) stands *šālēm yir'eh* as a cult aetiology of the name Jerusalem.

What are we to say about this? It is certainly true that a better case for the identification of 'the land of Moriah . . . upon one of the mountains' (Gen. 22.2) with Jerusalem can be made than is often assumed. The evidence of 2 Chron. 3.1 should not be set aside cavalierly as simply a late identification by the Chronicler,[134] since Gen. 22.14 itself locates the scene 'on the mount of the Lord', a term strongly suggestive of Jerusalem. Apart from one occasion when the expression is used of Gibeon (2 Sam. 21.6, LXX, cf. v. 9) and a few times when Sinai is intended, which latter does not seem likely here, the expression 'mount of the Lord' is always applied in the Old Testament to Jerusalem. This point is not mentioned by Stolz. However, it does not appear that the story in Gen. 22 relates to the Molech cult. It is true that it is in origin an aetiological story encouraging the abolition of human sacrifice, even though in its present context it serves rather as a test of Abraham's faith with regard to Yahweh's promise about his descendants (cf. Gen. 21.12, etc.). However, the deity in question is Yahweh, and we have seen above that Yahweh is not to be equated with Molech. Furthermore, the cult site in Gen. 22 coheres with this conclusion, since, if it were a

132 Cf. A. S. Kapelrud, 'King and fertility. A discussion of II Sam 21.1–14' in *Interpretationes ad Vetus Testamentum pertinentes Sigmundo Mowinckel septuagenario missae* (Oslo, 1955), pp. 113–22, and H. Cazelles, 'David's monarchy and the Gibeonite claim', *PEQ* 87 (1955), 165–75.

133 *Strukturen und Figuren im Kult von Jerusalem* (*BZAW* 118, 1970), pp. 207f.

134 Cf. J. Skinner, *A Critical and Exegetical Commentary on Genesis* (Edinburgh, 1910), p. 328.

question of an aetiological story specifically encouraging the abolition of the Molech cult, we should naturally expect the scene to be set in the valley of Hinnom. It therefore seems that the story in Gen. 22 originally served as an aetiology for the abolition of human sacrifice to Yahweh and was not specifically directed at the Molech cult. Finally, it may be noted that it is unnecessary to suppose that Shalem is to be understood as lying behind Yahweh in the expression *yahweh yir'eh* in Gen. 22.14 in order to provide a satisfactory aetiology. Rather, one should perhaps compare the words, 'as it is said to this day, "On the mount of the Lord he will be seen" ', with Ps. 84.8 (ET 7), where we read that 'the God of gods[135] will be seen in Zion'.

In conclusion, it may be confidently asserted that the Molech sacrifices are not to be equated with the offering of the first-born to Yahweh, and in any case, Molech was not equated with Yahweh, though there were those who worshipped both gods, and so may well have believed that Yahweh approved of the Molech sacrifices.

135 Reading *'ēl 'elōhīm* for MT *'el -'elōhīm*, supported by LXX, Aquila and the Peshiṭta. The MT's reading may have been occasioned by a desire to avoid the idea of Yahweh's being seen (cf. Exod. 33.20). Some scholars go further and suppose that MT *yērā'eh* is a deliberate alteration of *yir'ū*, in which case the original rendering would be even starker, 'they shall see the God of gods in Zion'.

4

Passages where allusions to Molech have sometimes wrongly been found

2 Samuel 12.31

This verse is a well-known crux, although it is now generally thought that it alludes to David's putting the defeated Ammonites to forced labour rather than torturing them. The words with which we are especially concerned, which appear in the MT as *wᵉheʿᵉḇîr ʾōṯām bammalkēn* (the last word being *kethibh*), have occasionally been thought to refer to the Molech cult. Thus Ḳimḥi renders them as 'he made them pass through Malchan, i.e. through the place where the Ammonites used to burn their sons to their idol'. In the nineteenth century, O. Thenius,[1] who noted this passage in Ḳimḥi, suggested that *bammalkēn* was originally *bᵉmolkām* or *bammilkōm*, thus yielding the translation 'he offered (burned) them in their Molech (image)' or 'he offered (burned) them in the Molech image'.[2] This was criticized by C. F. Keil[3] on the grounds that it involved arbitrary emendation of the text and that the expression *heʿᵉḇîr bammōleḵ* is essentially different from *heʿᵉḇîr bāʾēš lammōleḵ*, the phrase used elsewhere in connection with Molech. Also, he pointed out that it was hard to see how Thenius could claim that David's action represented a striking victory over idolatry, since in offering up the Ammonites in this way he was perpetuating the Molech cult.

Others, for example A. F. Kirkpatrick,[4] accepted the reading of the *qere bammalbēn* instead of the *kethibh bammalkēn*, and rendered 'and he made them pass through the *brick-kiln*' and thought that the phrase was chosen with reference to the Ammonite practice of passing children through the fire to Molech.

More recently, however, another scholar, G. C. O'Ceallaigh,[5] has

1 *Die Bücher Samuels* (Leipzig, 1842), p. 182.
2 Cf. below, p. 88, n. 6 on the image of Molech.
3 *Biblischer Commentar über die prophetischen Geschichtsbücher des Alten Testaments* (Leipzig, 1875), p. 308.
4 *The Second Book of Samuel* (Cambridge, 1899), p. 134.
5 '"And *so* David did to *all the cities* of Ammon"', *VT* 12 (1962), 179–89.

sought to find a direct reference to Molech in this verse. He translates the passage as 'and he made them desecrate (or, demolish) the Molechs', reading *bmlkn* with the *kethibh* but vocalizing it as *bammālᵉḵīn*. He claims that *mālᵉḵīn* is the plural of the Aramaic *pᵉʿal* participial noun *mālēḵ* and suggests two reasons why this curious form should be used here: (i) the Aramaic plural was used in order to make it clear that it is an idol and not earthly kings that is involved here; (ii) the plural form was also employed to express contempt for the idol: 'Yahweh was one, but of this heathen Baal there were many.' He further suggests that the verb *hʿbyr* was chosen for its ironical effect, since it was also used in connection with the offerings to Molech.

All these views must certainly be rejected, since, as we have seen, it was not Molech but Milcom who was the god of Ammon, and the Old Testament clearly distinguishes them. More specifically, objections to the view of Thenius have already been noted. Ḳimḥi introduces an unnecessary *hapax legomenon*, and O'Ceallaigh produces a previously unattested plural form of Molech, which also has the oddity of being in Aramaic. As for Kirkpatrick, he, like many other scholars, is surely right in following the *qere* reading *malbēn* rather than the *kethibh malkēn*, but as G. Hoffmann[6] had already shown in 1882, there is no evidence that it means 'brick-kiln' either in the ancient Versions or in Semitic philology. Rather, the evidence of post-biblical Hebrew and Arabic and Syriac cognates supports the meaning 'brick-mould'. Since it makes no sense to say that David 'passed them through the brick-mould', it seems better to follow Hoffmann and many others subsequently[7] and accept the easy emendation of *wᵉheʿᵉḇīr* to *wᵉheʿᵉḇīḏ* and translate 'and he made them work at the brick-moulds'. Since *śīm bᵉ* can mean 'to set, appoint to' (cf. 1 Sam. 8.11), the verse can be translated as a whole as follows: 'And he brought forth the people who were in it, and set them to labour with saws and iron picks and iron axes, and made them work at the brick-moulds; and thus he did to all the cities of the Ammonites.' There is no reference to torture in this verse, as is now generally accepted.[8] Nor, as we have seen, does the verse refer to Molech.

6 'Lexikalisches', *ZAW* 2 (1882), 53–72.

7 E.g. S. R. Driver, *Notes on the Hebrew Text of the Books of Samuel* (Oxford, 1890), pp. 226–9; E. Dhorme, *Les Livres de Samuel* (Paris, 1910), pp. 362f; P. K. McCarter, *II Samuel* (Garden City, 1984), pp. 310f; *RV* margin; *NAB*.

8 At this point one should note the article by J. F. A. Sawyer, 'David's treatment of the Ammonites (2 Samuel 12:31). – A study in the history of interpretation', *TGUOS* 26 (1975–6, but published 1979), 96–107. This contains a useful history of

1 Kings 11.7

As it stands the MT reads: 'Then Solomon built a high place for Kemosh the abomination of Moab, and for Molech the abomination of the Ammonites, on the mountain east of Jerusalem.' However, it is generally accepted that we should read Milcom instead of Molech (with the support of the Lucianic recension of the LXX and the Peshiṭta), since there stands against the MT the fact not merely that elsewhere the god of Ammon is spoken of as Milcom and that Milcom and Molech are clearly distinguished (cf. 2 Kgs. 23.10, 13), but that in 1 Kgs. 11 itself, the same cult of the god of Ammon is referred to also in verses 5 and 33, and there the deity is called Milcom.[9] Similarly in 2 Kgs. 23.13, we have a reference back to Solomon's building of a high place to Milcom. All this strongly suggests that in 1 Kgs. 11.7, Molech is simply a slip for Milcom, the final *m* having fallen out.

Jeremiah 49.1, 3

Generally nowadays these two verses are rendered respectively as follows: verse 1, 'Concerning the Ammonites. Thus says the Lord: "Has Israel no sons? Has he no heir? Why then has Milcom dispossessed Gad, and his people settled in its cities"', and verse 3, 'Wail, O Heshbon, for Ai is laid waste! Cry, O daughters of Rabbah! Gird yourselves with sackcloth, lament, and run to and fro among the hedges! For Milcom shall go into exile, with his priests and his princes'. Although the MT reads *malkām* 'their king' in both verses 1 and 3, the LXX, Peshiṭta and Vulgate read Milcom. Geiger, O'Ceallaigh and Sabottka,[10] however, prefer to read 'their Molech' or 'their Melek', but as has been emphasized earlier, there is no reason to believe that Molech was regarded as the god of the

the interpretation of the verse. It also puts forward the suggestion that the text originally read *wayyāśem bamm^{e}gērāh ūḇammalbēn* 'and he set them to work with stone-saws and brick-moulds' but that the Deuteronomist in the exile, inspired by anti-Ammonite feeling, interpolated words about David's savagery (including *w^{e}he$^{\text{ʿ}e}$ḇīr*). This, however, seems unduly speculative.

9 On the possible ultimate connection between Molech and Milcom, cf. above, pp. 32–3, 47.

10 A. Geiger, *Urschrift und Uebersetzungen der Bibel* (Breslau, 1857), p. 306; O'Ceallaigh, '"And *so* David did to *all the cities* of Ammon"', p. 186, n. 1; L. Sabottka, *Zephanja, Versuch einer Neuübersetzung mit philologischem Kommentar* (Rome, 1972), pp. 37–8, reads 'ihr Melek' in v. 3 but does not discuss v. 1.

Ammonites, since the latter is called Milcom and distinguished from the Canaanite god Molech. There are, however, two good reasons why we should read Milcom rather than *malkām* 'their king' in Jer. 49.1, 3. First, with regard to Jer. 49.1, if we read 'their king', the context demands that this should refer to the king of Ammonites, but this does not agree with the immediate antecedent, which is Israel. There is no such problem if we read Milcom, and from this it also becomes natural to read Milcom rather than 'their king' in verse 3. Secondly, in favour of seeing Milcom in verse 3 is the very similar verse concerning Moab in Jer. 48.7, 'and Kemosh[11] shall go into exile, with his priests and his princes'. (On Amos 1.15, which has clearly influenced Jer. 49.3, see below, pp. 77–8.)

Molech in Hosea?

There are a number of references in Hosea which have mostly been thought of as referring to the Israelite 'king', but which a few scholars have believed allude rather to a deity Melek, i.e. Molech. This view seems first to have been adumbrated by Geiger[12] in the nineteenth century, but in the present century it has been advanced in particular by H. S. Nyberg.[13] It has also been followed by another Scandinavian, G. Östborn,[14] and in a couple of instances by H. Cazelles.[15] The passages in question are the following, in which I here append the usual renderings:

Hos. 3.4: For the children of Israel shall dwell many days without king or prince, without sacrifice or pillar, without ephod or teraphim.

Hos. 5.13: When Ephraim saw his sickness, and Judah his wound,
then Ephraim went to Assyria, and sent to the great king.
But he is not able to cure you or heal your wounds.

Hos. 7.3: By their wickedness they make the king glad, and the princes by their treachery.

Hos. 7.5: On the day of our king the princes became sick with the heat of wine;
he stretched out his hand with mockers.

11 Reading *ḵ^e^mōš* with the *qere* and many manuscripts instead of *ḵ^e^mîš* (*kethibh*).
12 *Urschrift*, p. 307.
13 *Studien zum Hoseabuche* (Uppsala, 1935), *passim*.
14 *Yahweh and Baal: Studies in the Book of Hosea and Related Documents* (Lund, 1956), pp. 7, 23, 34, 38, 42, 55–7, 81, 103.
15 'The problem of the kings in Osee, viii 4', *CBQ* 11 (1949), 14–25.

Hos. 8.4: They made kings, but not through me; they appointed princes but without my knowledge.

Hos. 8.10: Though they hire allies among the nations, I will soon gather them up.
And they shall cease for a little while from anointing king and princes.[16]

Hos. 10.3: For now they will say: 'We have no king,
We fear not the Lord, and a king, what could he do for us?'

Hos. 10.6: Yea, the thing itself shall be carried to Assyria, as tribute to the great king.

Hos. 10.7: Samaria's king shall perish, like a chip on the face of the waters.

Hos. 10.15: Thus I shall do[17] to you, O house of Israel,[18] because of your great wickedness.
At dawn the king of Israel shall be utterly cut off.

Hos. 13.10: Where[19] now is your king, to save you in all your cities,
and your judges of whom you said, 'give me a king and princes'?

The overwhelming majority of scholars, however, have remained unconvinced that a deity Melek (Molech) is referred to in any of these passages and continue to translate simply 'king', as in the renderings given above.[20] Since *meleḵ* occurs so many times in the Old Testament with the ordinary meaning 'king' and is only occasionally attested as the name of a deity, the onus of proof is clearly on those who wish to find examples of the latter here. But all the passages are more naturally understood against the background of the last years of the Northern Kingdom when king followed king in quick succession as one *coup d'état* followed another, rather than as allusions to a god. If it were a question of Molech, we should expect allusions to human sacrifice alongside the references, but this is

16 This translation follows the LXX, reading *wᵉyeḥdᵉlū mᵉʿaṭ mimmᵉšōaḥ meleḵ wᵉśārīm* in the second half of the verse instead of MT's *wayyāḥēllū mᵉʿāṭ mimmaśśāʾ meleḵ śārīm*.

17 Reading *ʾeʿᵉśeh* 'I shall do' for MT *ʿāśāh* 'he has done', with the support of LXX. Another proposal is to read *yēʿāśeh* 'it shall be done'.

18 The MT has a reference to the place name Bethel, but it is preferable to read *bēṯ yiśrāʾēl* 'house of Israel' with the LXX. Not only does this fit the context better but Hosea elsewhere refers to Bethel rather as *bēṯ ʾāwen* (apart from Hos. 12.5, ET 4, which is understandable).

19 We should either emend *ʾᵉhī* to *ʾayyēh* 'where' or regard it as a dialectal variant of the latter (cf. v. 14 and the ancient Versions).

20 A glance at the main commentaries on Hosea will confirm this, e.g. those by H. W. Wolff, W. Rudolph, J. L. Mays, and F. I. Andersen and D. N. Freedman. A useful study of these passages will be found in A. Gelston, 'Kingship in the book of Hosea', *OTS* 19 (1974), 71–85, with criticism of Nyberg on pp. 72–3.

nowhere the case.[21] Furthermore, 'princes' (understood by Nyberg as mythical deities alongside Melek) are nowhere else mentioned in connection with Molech in the Old Testament, and are perfectly understandable as princes of the court at Samaria (Hos. 3.4, 7.3, 5, 8.10, 13.10). To take but two examples, the references to 'king and princes' in Hos. 7.3, 5 cannot be dissociated from the allusion to the kings in Hos. 7.7, 'All of them are hot as an oven, and they devour their rulers. All their kings have fallen; and none of them calls upon me'. This cannot refer to anything but the earthly kings in Samaria, and similar non-divine references must therefore be intended by the 'king and princes' in Hos. 7.3, 5, and surely in the other passages as well. Although less decisive as arguments, the points may also be made that the Old Testament nowhere else alludes to the Molech cult in connection with the Northern Kingdom and neither the MT nor any of the ancient Versions perceived allusions to Molech in Hosea.

Nyberg[22] claims that Melek in Hos. 5.13 must be a god, since the people resort to him for healing, which in Hos. 6.1 and 11.3 is a function of Yahweh. This is not a compelling argument, however, since this language might equally have been applied to an earthly king, and, in any case, the parallelism with Assyria (cf. Hos. 10.6) would suggest that if Melek were here a god, it would be Assyrian, which cannot be true of Molech. Cazelles,[23] it is true, finds Melek to be an allusion to the Assyrian god Ashur in Hos. 5.13, 8.4 and 8.10, in which case there would be no connection with Molech. It is, however, unlikely that Hosea's allusions to the 'king' ever refer to a god and much more natural to suppose that a political reference is intended.

Amos 1.15

This verse, part of Amos' oracle against the Ammonites, has generally been translated: ' "and their king shall go into exile, he and his princes together", says the Lord'. Geiger, O'Ceallaigh and

21 It has sometimes been supposed that there is a reference to human sacrifice in Hos. 13:2b. However, not only is there no reference to Molech or Melek here, but it is also doubtful whether there is any allusion to human sacrifice either. The MT admittedly reads, 'Those who sacrifice (*zōḇ*^{e}*ḥē*) men kiss calves', and this is still favoured by some commentators such as H. W. Wolff and F. I. Andersen and D. N. Freedman (*ad loc.*). However, Hosea makes no other allusions to human sacrifice and such an intrusion seems improbable in the present context. Since the LXX, Symmachus, Aquila, Theodotion and the Vulgate support the emendation of *zōb*^{e}*ḥē* to *ziḇ*^{e}*ḥū*, we should probably render 'Sacrifice (*ziḇ*^{e}*ḥū*) to these, they say. Men kiss calves!', as is widely held.

22 *Studien zum Hoseabuche*, p. 39.

23 'The problem of Kings', pp. 21f, 24.

Sabottka,[24] however, believe that *malkām* should here be read 'their Molech' or 'their Melek' rather than 'their king', but this is completely unjustified, since there is no evidence that Molech was the god of the Ammonites, namely Milcom. It has, indeed, been suggested that we read Milcom rather than 'their king' here, for example by M. J. Mulder,[25] and this is supported by certain manuscripts of the LXX, especially those of the Lucianic group, by Aquila and Symmachus, all of which read *Μελχομ*, and by the Vulgate, which reads Melchom. It is, moreover, worthy of note that in Jer. 49.3, a passage clearly dependent on Amos 1.15, we should certainly read Milcom rather than 'their king'. However, it does not automatically follow from this that we should likewise read Milcom in Amos 1.15: it is not unknown for one Old Testament text dependent on another to contain an element of reinterpretation, whether conscious or not. That this is the case here, and that 'their king' rather than Milcom is to be read, gains in probability when we recall that none of the other oracles against foreign nations in Amos mentions the god of the nation in question, whereas all the other foreign nation oracles whose authenticity is probable allude to the coming judgment on the ruler (cf. Amos 1.5, 8, 2.3).

Amos 2.1

Traditionally the words of this verse have been rendered: 'Thus says the Lord: "For three transgressions of Moab, and for four, I will not revoke the punishment; because he burned to lime the bones of the king of Edom."' However, N. H. Tur-Sinai (H. Torczyner),[26] with characteristic audacity, has proposed that instead of *meleḵ ʾᵉḏōm laśśîḏ* 'the king of Edom . . . to lime', we should read *mōleḵ ʾāḏām lᵉšōḏ* 'a human sacrifice out of violence', so that the last part of the verse should be translated, 'for he burned the bones of a human sacrifice out of violence'. W. F. Albright[27] accepted this, except that he suggested reading *laššēḏ* for MT *laśśîḏ* (cf. Ps. 106.37), and thus rendered the last part of the verse as 'because he burns the bones of a human sacrifice to a demon'. This whole suggestion is, however,

24 Geiger, *Urschrift*, p. 306, takes *malkām*, to refer to Molech, O'Ceallaigh, '"And *so* David did to *all the cities* of Ammon"', p. 186, n. 1, renders 'their Molech', and Sabottka, *Zephanja*, pp. 37–8, finds a reference to the god Melek here.

25 *Kanaänitische goden in het Oude Testament* (The Hague, 1965), p. 57.

26 הלשון והספר, vol. 1 (Jerusalem, 1948), pp. 64–70.

27 *Yahweh and the Gods of Canaan* (London, 1968), p. 209.

extremely dubious. It will be noted that *mlk ʾdm* is here understood in the same sense as Punic *mlk ʾdm* 'sacrifice of a man'. The views of Tur-Sinai and Albright should be rejected because (a) there is no evidence that *mlk* in the Old Testament – in contrast to Punic – is ever a sacrificial term, and (b) their views involve emendation of the MT without versional support, when it makes perfectly good sense as it stands.

Amos 5.26

A number of scholars have seen a reference to Molech in this verse.[28] Unlike almost all the other passages considered in this section, the allusion to Molech is already attested in the LXX which reads, 'And you took up the tent of Moloch, and the star of your god Raiphan, the images of them which you made for yourselves'. This verse is cited in the New Testament in Stephen's speech in Acts 7.43, except that instead of the words 'of your god Raiphan' we read 'of the god Rompha', or alternatively Romphan or Rempham, and the variants Remphan, Rempha, Raiphan, Rephan, Repha, Reaphan and Raphan are also attested. Also, instead of 'which you made for yourselves', the version in Acts reads 'which you made to worship'. Raiphan in the LXX rendering is clearly a corruption of Kaiwan (MT *kiyyūn*) and Moloch corresponds to MT *malk*ᵉ*ḵem* 'your king'. But does this actually allude to the god Molech?

This verse is a well-known crux. As it stands the MT reads: 'And you shall take up Sikkuth your king, and Kiyyun your images, the star of your god which you made for yourselves.' Some scholars[29] emend *sikkūṯ* to *sukkaṯ* 'booth' and understand *kīyyūn* as 'pedestal', thus rendering 'You shall take up the booth of your king, and the pedestal of your images'. However, the words 'the star of your god' (*kôḵaḇ* ᵉ*lōhēḵem*) which follow in this verse, and which are probably an explanatory gloss, support the majority of scholars who prefer to see here an allusion to *kēwān* 'Saturn' rather than *kīyyūn* 'pedestal' (cf. Akkadian *kayyamānu*, Arabic and Persian *kaywān*, Syriac

28 E.g. Geiger, *Urschrift*, p. 306; O'Ceallaigh, '"And *so* David did to *all the cities* of Ammon"', p. 186, n. 2; S. Gevirtz, 'A new look at an old crux: Amos 5 26', *JBL* 87 (1968), 267–76; M. Weinfeld, 'The worship of Molech and of the Queen of Heaven and its background', *UF* 4 (1972), pp. 149f. O'Ceallaigh translates 'your Molech' and Gevirtz renders 'your (god) MLK', both of which are contrary to Hebrew grammar, since a proper name should not take a possessive suffix.

29 Cf. especially W. R. Harper, *A Critical and Exegetical Commentary on Amos and Hosea* (Edinburgh, 1905), pp. 137–8.

kēʾwān, all meaning 'Saturn').[30] The MT pointing of *kēwān* as *kīyyūn* must reflect the vowels of the Hebrew word *šiqqūṣ* 'abomination', and it is therefore plausible to suppose that the expression *sikkūṯ* similarly has distorted vocalization, concealing the name of an idolatrous deity.[31] It has been common to suppose that the word was originally vocalized Sakkuth (*sakkūṯ*)[32] and it is usual to think that this is another name for Saturn, on the basis of the Šurpu tablets, where it has been believed that *Sag-kud* and *kayyamānu* are associated.[33] However, R. Borger[34] has recently shown that the correct reading (Šurpu, tablet II, line 80) is ^{d}*Sag-kud* ^{d}*Nita*, not ^{d}*Sag-kud* ^{d}*kayyamānu*, so that evidence that *Sag-kud* denotes Saturn is lacking. However, whatever 'Sakkuth (?) your king' refers to precisely, there is no particular reason to find here an allusion to Molech.[35]

Amos 7.13

Traditionally the words of the priest Amaziah to Amos the prophet in this verse have been rendered, 'but never again prophesy at Bethel, for it is the king's sanctuary, and it is a temple of the kingdom'. W. C. Wood,[36] however, proposed that *miqdaš-meleḵ* should be translated 'sanctuary of ham-Melek' rather than 'the king's sanctuary', and he made it clear that he equates this deity with Molech. However, he gave no supporting evidence for this view, and indeed there is none. It is much more natural to give *meleḵ* its normal meaning 'king', which fits the context admirably, as the preceding verses have been concerned with Amos' preaching against the king, Jeroboam II (cf.

30 Cf. S. R. Driver, *The Books of Joel and Amos*, 2nd edn (Cambridge, 1915), pp. 192–3; J. L. Mays, *Amos* (London, 1969), p. 112; E. Hammershaimb, *The Book of Amos. A Commentary* (ET, Oxford, 1970), pp. 92–3; H. W. Wolff, *Dodekapropheton 2 Joel und Amos*, 2nd edn (Neukirchen-Vluyn, 1969), p. 304 (ET, *Joel and Amos* [Philadelphia, 1977], p. 260). Interestingly the Peshiṭta reads *kēʾwān* 'Saturn' here. In the pre-critical period Ibn Ezra also saw an allusion to Saturn here.

31 The suggestion that the pointing of *sikkūṯ* (as also of *kīyyūn*) in the MT reflects the vocalization of the Hebrew word *šiqqūṣ* 'abomination' was first put forward by C. C. Torrey, 'On the text of Amos v. 26; vi. 1. 2; vii. 2', *JBL* 13 (1894), 61f.

32 See n. 30 (the citations of modern literature).

33 Cf. E. Reiner, *Šurpu. A Collection of Sumerian and Akkadian Incantations* (*Archiv für Orientforschung Beiheft* 11, 1958), p. 18, tablet, II, line 180.

34 'Amos 5, 26, Apostelgeschichte 7, 43 und Šurpu II, 180', *ZAW* 100 (1988), 70–81.

35 C. D. Isbell, 'Another look at Amos 5:26', *JBL* 97 (1978), 97–9, sees a reference to Milcom here, which involves deleting one of the *k*'s owing to dittography. However, since Isbell also sees a reference to the Assyrian deity Kaiwan in this verse, it is surprising to find a reference to the Ammonite god Milcom in parallelism with it. Furthermore, there is no versional support in favour of reading Milcom.

36 'The religion of Canaan (concluded)', *JBL* 35 (1916), 257.

vv. 9, 10, 11, esp. v. 9, where Amos proclaims judgment on both the sanctuaries [*miqd^{e}šē*] of Israel and the house of Jeroboam). Furthermore, there is no evidence that Molech had a sanctuary at Bethel, for elsewhere in the Old Testament we find him associated with the cult site in the valley of Hinnom by Jerusalem.

SUMMARY AND CONCLUSIONS

Until 1935 it was universally held that Molech in the Old Testament was the name of a god. In that year, however, Eissfeldt argued that Old Testament *mōleḵ* is rather the name of a type of sacrifice, like the Punic word *mlk*. That Punic *mlk* is a sacrificial term (root *hlk* 'to go', rather than cognate with Syriac *m^{e}laḵ* as Eissfeldt thought) is correct: the meaning 'king' supported by Weinfeld and others is inappropriate in a number of contexts. On the other hand, Old Testament *mōleḵ* is certainly the name of a god, not a sacrificial term. One does not go awhoring after a sacrifice (Lev. 20.5), the construction *he'^{e}ḇīr l^e* + *mōleḵ* may be paralleled by other instances of *he'^{e}ḇīr l^e* + divine name, and there is no support in the ancient Versions for the sacrificial understanding of Molech. Also to be rejected is the view that *mōleḵ* was a sacrificial term in origin but was misunderstood as a divine name by the Old Testament. To maintain this view involves the unlikely assumption that not one but several writers all misunderstood it, some of whom should certainly have been in a good position to know its meaning. Moreover, there is extra-biblical evidence for the existence of a god Molech.

Explicit references to the Molech cult are to be found in Lev. 18.21, 20.2–5; Jer. 32.35 and 2 Kgs. 23.10. Implicit references are to be found in a number of other passages (e.g. Isa. 30.33, 57.9; Jer. 7.31, 19.5, and perhaps Zeph. 1.5), including one passage which has hitherto remained undetected (Isa. 28.15, 18). Alleged references to Molech which are in fact untenable (discussed in a concluding chapter) are in 2 Sam. 12.31; 1 Kgs. 11.7; Jer. 49.1, 3; Hos. 3.4, 5.13, 7.3, 5, 8.4, 10, 10.3, 6, 7, 15, 13.10; Amos 1.15, 2.1, 5.26 and 7.13.

With regard to the question whether the Molech cult involved human sacrifice or simply dedication in the fire, some scholars deny that even the Old Testament itself speaks of sacrifice. But this is to overlook the evidence of the text itself, which clearly speaks of burning (Jer. 7.31, 19.5, cf. 32.35). Moreover, in Isa. 30.33 imagery is taken up from the Molech cult and applied to the coming destruction of the Assyrians, which confirms the sacrificial interpretation but does not fit the dedicatory view. Other scholars admit that the Old Testament itself speaks of human sacrifice in connection with Molech but think that it is exaggerating. Far-flung anthropological parallels are sometimes preferred as evidence to the testimony of the biblical text itself. However, there is evidence in classical and Punic sources, as well as archaeological evidence, for the existence of human sacrifice elsewhere in the Canaanite world, and so there is no reason to doubt the Old Testament allusions. (Translations of the classical passages may be found in the appendix.) The expression *heʿᵉḇîr (bāʾēš)*, often rendered 'he passed . . . (through the fire)' seems to have misled some scholars into thinking that human sacrifice was not involved. However, the expression clearly has sacrificial connotations (cf. Exod. 13.12f, where *hʿbyr=zbḥ* 'sacrifice' and Ezek. 20.25–6, where *hʿbyr* used of human beings is said to be horrifying). It is therefore clear that the rabbinic interpretation by which the Molech cult simply involved dedication to idolatry is wrong.

Another rabbinic view understood giving one's seed to Molech (Lev. 18.21) as an allusion to mixed marriages, which led to idolatry. Lev. 18.21 is set in a context of prohibited sexual relations and this has led some modern scholars also to see the Molech cult as having a sexual element. However, in view of the parallel passage in Lev. 20.5 which applies sexual language to the Molech cult in a spiritualized sense ('playing the harlot after Molech'; cf. too Ps. 106:37–9; Ezek. 23.37), it seems likely that the sexual context of the Molech prohibition in Lev. 18.21 is to be understood in the same way.

The Molech sacrifices were offered in the valley of Hinnom, just outside Jerusalem, at the Topheth. This word is cognate with Aramaic *tap̱yā* and Syriac *tᵉp̱ayā* (and *tᵉp̱āyā*) meaning 'fire-place', 'oven' or 'furnace'. It has sometimes been supposed that the word is cognate with Hebrew *špt*, a verb used of setting a pot on the fire in 2 Kgs. 4.38 and Ezek. 24.3, and *ʾašp̱ōṯ* 'ashes'; and as Hebrew *š* may be equivalent to Aramaic *t*, it has been supposed that the word Topheth is an Aramaic loan-word. Topheth is certainly cognate with Aramaic *tap̱yā* and Syriac *tᵉp̱ayā* (*tᵉp̱āyā*), since the meaning 'fire-place' fits it perfectly (cf. Isa. 30.33). However, since it appears that *tap̱yā* and *tᵉp̱ayā* (*tᵉp̱āyā*) are formations from the verb 'to bake' (in Hebrew *ʾph*), Topheth cannot also be cognate with *špt*, a quite different verb, which, in any case, means simply 'to set' without specific fiery associations (cf. Ps. 22.16, ET 15). Nor is it cognate with *ʾašpōṯ*, which means 'dung' rather than 'ashes'. Topheth is therefore not an Aramaic loan-word. The fact that the Old Testament repeatedly makes clear that the Molech cult was Canaanite, not Aramean, would in any case render this improbable.

Who, then, was Molech? Many Old Testament references imply the Canaanite origin of his cult. This alone might serve to refute the equation of Molech with the Ammonite god Milcom (though there may have been some ultimate connection) or the Aramean deity Adad-milki, views which are in any case open to objection on other grounds. Nor is Molech to be equated with Baal:[1] the two are clearly distinguished (cf. 2 Kgs. 23.5, 10). Indeed, it is difficult to believe that we have to do with any other god than one whose proper name was *mlk*, presumably properly vocalized *Meleḵ* (or *Mōlēḵ*) in Hebrew, since it may be granted that one of the vowels of the form Molech has been tampered with, reflecting the word *bōšeṯ* 'shame'. That there was indeed a Canaanite god *mlk* is proved by two Ugaritic serpent charms (*Ugaritica* V. 7[*RS* 24.244=*KTU* 1.100], line 41 and *Ugaritica* V. 8 [*RS* 24.251=*KTU* 1.107], line 17) which mention him. In Akkadian sources this deity is called Malik and we find him equated with the underworld god Nergal. This fits Old Testament Molech perfectly, since there are reasons for believing that he was an underworld deity. Thus Isa. 57.9 reads: 'You journeyed to Molech with oil and multiplied your perfumes; you sent your envoys far off, and sent down even to Sheol.' On the most natural interpretation this locates Molech in Sheol. Moreover, the fact that Gehenna (a name deriving from the Aramaic word for 'valley of Hinnom') became a term for the fiery underworld is understandable if the valley of Hinnom was the seat of an underworld cult. It is of interest to note that, in Job 18.13–14, Death is called 'the king of terrors', and in the Koran Mālik appears as an underworld angel, though the latter is admittedly late. Moreover, the allusion to the rulers of Jerusalem making a covenant with Death and Sheol in order to avert the Assyrian threat (Isa. 28.15,

1 On the other hand, it is argued that the god to whom the Punic human sacrifices were offered, Baal-ḥammon, is to be equated with Baal and not El, as is usually supposed. Sometimes, indeed, he is simply called Baal, whereas he is never called El. His consort, Tinnit, is fused with Astarte in a Phoenician text from Sarepta, and Astarte is known to have been the wife of Baal. Finally, it should be noted that the fact that classical sources almost always refer to the Punic deity as Kronos (Saturn) does not prove that he was El, for there is evidence that Kronos could denote Baal as well as El, and in Polybius Baal-ḥammon is actually named Zeus, the usual equivalent of Baal.

18) makes sense as an allusion to the Molech cult. The most common view is that the passage refers to an alliance with Egypt or to a Mot cult, but scholars are at a loss to explain satisfactorily why Egypt should be called Death or Sheol, and no Mot cult in Judah is otherwise known at this time.

Was Molech equated with Yahweh? Often it has been thought so. In particular, three references in Jeremiah (from the Deuteronomistic redactor) have been cited in which Yahweh claims that he had not commanded the Israelites to offer up their children in sacrifice (Jer. 7.31, 19.5, 32.35), which might suggest that some people maintained that he had. Some further suppose that this is to be correlated with the commandment in the Pentateuch to offer up the first-born to Yahweh. However, similar language is employed in Deut. 17.3, where Yahweh declares that he had not commanded the people to worship the sun, the moon and the host of heaven, yet no one supposes that anyone equated Yahweh with these heavenly beings. In both cases we need assume no more than that some people thought of Yahweh as approving the cults in question. Moreover, if, as has been argued, Molech was an underworld god, it is inherently unlikely that Yahweh would have been equated with him, since Yahweh seems to have been rather separated from the underworld through long periods of Israel's history. Further, the fact that the Molech cult did not take place in Yahweh's temple in Jerusalem, but in a separate site in the valley of Hinnom, suggests that we have to do with different deities.

Nor is it possible to equate the human sacrifices offered to Molech with the first-born offered to Yahweh, since (a) the first-born are never specifically mentioned in connection with Molech, but rather we hear of children generally, and (b) both boys and girls are said to have been offered to Molech but the law of the first-born involved only boys. Again, it may be noted that Gen. 22 in its original intention cannot have been an aetiological story specifically directed against the Molech cult, since the location of the intended sacrifice there is not the Hinnom valley but rather one of the mountains of Moriah, i.e. probably Zion (v. 2, cf. v. 14 and 2 Chron. 3.1). Gen. 22 is rather to be seen as directed against the offering of human sacrifice to Yahweh.

APPENDIX

Classical and patristic references to Phoenician and Carthaginian human sacrifice[1]

Phoenician human sacrifice

QUINTUS CURTIUS, *HISTORY OF ALEXANDER* IV.3.23. 'Some even proposed renewing a sacrifice which had been discontinued for many years, and which I for my part should believe to be by no means pleasing to the gods, of offering a freeborn boy to Saturn – this sacrilege rather than sacrifice, handed down from their founders, the Carthaginians are said to have performed until the destruction of their city – and unless the elders, in accordance with whose counsel everything was done, had opposed it, the awful superstition would have prevailed over mercy.'[2]

PHILO OF BYBLOS (CITED BY EUSEBIUS, *PRAEPARATIO EVANGELICA* I.10.45, and again almost identically in IV.16.11). 'It was a custom of the ancients in great crises of danger for the rulers of a city or nation, in order to avert the common ruin, to give up the most beloved of their children for sacrifice as a ransom to the avenging daemons: and those who were thus given up were sacrificed with mystic rites. Kronos then, whom the Phoenicians call Elus, who was king of the country and subsequently, after his decease, was deified as the star Saturn, had by a nymph of the country named Anobret an only begotten son, whom they on this account called Iedud, the only begotten being still so called among the Phoenicians; and when very great dangers from war had beset the country, he arrayed his son in royal apparel, and prepared an altar, and sacrificed him.'[3]

1 Translations are my own except where otherwise stated.
2 Translation is from J. C. Rolfe (ed.), *Quintus Curtius* (Loeb Classical Library, London and Cambridge, Mass., 1946), p. 195.
3 Translation is from E. H. Gifford (ed.), *Eusebii Pamphili evangelicae praeparationis*, vol. 3, pt. 1 (Oxford, 1903), p. 171.

PORPHYRY, *DE ABSTINENTIA* II.56 (ALSO CITED BY EUSEBIUS, *PRAEPARATIO EVANGELICA* IV.16.6). 'The Phoenicians, too, in the great calamities of war, or pestilence, or drought, used to dedicate one of their dearest friends and sacrifice him to Kronos: and of those who thus sacrificed the Phoenician history is full, which Sanchuniathon wrote in the Phoenician language, and Philo Byblius translated into Greek in eight books.'[4]

Carthaginian human sacrifice[5]

SOPHOCLES, *ANDROMEDA*, FRAGMENT 122. 'There is amongst the barbarians a law which from olden times prescribes the offering of a human sacrifice to Kronos.'

PSEUDO-PLATO, *MINOS* 315E. 'Amongst us there is not a law prescribing human sacrifices: on the contrary, this would be abominable; whilst the Carthaginians perform such sacrifices as something sacred and lawful, and certain among them even go as far as sacrificing their own sons to Kronos, as you too could have heard.'

KLEITARCHOS, SCHOLIA ON PLATO'S *REPUBLIC* 337A. 'Kleitarchos says the Phoenicians and especially the Carthaginians who honoured Kronos, whenever they wished to succeed in any great enterprise, would vow by one of their children if they achieved the things they longed for, to sacrifice him to the god. A bronze image of Kronos was set up among them, stretching out its cupped hands above a bronze cauldron, which would burn the child. As the flame of the burning child surrounded the body, the limbs would shrivel up and the mouth would appear to grin as if laughing, until it was shrunk enough to slip into the cauldron.'

ENNIUS, *ANNALS*, FRAGMENT 221 (Book VII). 'The Carthaginians are accustomed to sacrifice their little boys to the gods.'

DIONYSIUS OF HALICARNASSUS I.38. 'They say that the ancients used to offer to Kronos human victims, just as at Carthage so long as the city existed, and as the Celts and some other western nations still do today.'

4 Translation is from *ibid.*, p. 45, cf. pp. 171f.

5 For classical citations regarding Carthaginian human sacrifice cf. M. Mayer, 'Kronos' in W. H. Roscher (ed.), *Ausführliches Lexikon der griechischen und römischen Mythologie*, vol. 2 (Leipzig, 1890–7), cols. 1501–3; M. Leglay, *Saturne Africain. Histoire* (Paris, 1966), pp. 315–19.

DIODORUS SICULUS XIII.86.3. 'Among the dead was also Hannibal the general, and among the watch-guards who were sent out there were some who reported that in the night spirits of the dead were to be seen. Himilcar, on seeing how the throng was beset with superstitious fear, first of all put a stop to the destruction of the monuments, and then he supplicated the gods after the custom of his people by sacrificing a young boy to Kronos and a multitude of cattle to Poseidon by drowning them in the sea.'

DIODORUS SICULUS XX.14.4–7. 'They also alleged that Kronos had turned against them inasmuch as in former times they had been accustomed to sacrifice to this god the noblest of their sons, but more recently, secretly buying and nurturing children, they had sent these to the sacrifice; and when an investigation was made, some of those who had been sacrificed were discovered to have been supposititious. When they had given thought to these things and saw their enemy encamped before their walls, they were filled with superstitious dread, for they believed that they had neglected the honours of the gods that had been established by their fathers. In their zeal to make amends for their omission, they selected two hundred of the noblest children and sacrificed them publicly; and others who were under suspicion sacrificed themselves voluntarily, in number not less than three hundred. There was in their city a bronze image of Kronos, extending its hands, palms up and sloping toward the ground, so that each of the children when placed thereon rolled down and fell into a sort of gaping pit filled with fire.[6] It is probable that it was from this that Euripides has drawn the mythical story found in his works about the sacrifice in Tauris, in which he presents Iphigeneia being asked by Orestes:

But what tomb shall receive me when I die?
A sacred fire within, and earth's broad rift.

Also the story passed down among the Greeks from ancient myth that Kronos did away with his own children appears to have been kept in mind among the Carthaginians through this observance.'[7]

6 The description of the idol of Kronos here (apparently going back to Kleitarchos; also cf. Plutarch, *De Superstitione* 13) is strikingly similar to the description of the idol of Molech in certain rabbinic sources, i.e. Ēchā rabbāthī on Lam. 1.9 and Yalḳūṭ on Jer. 7.31 (the latter quoted from Midrash Yelammedēnu, cf. S. Buber (ed.), *Midrasch Tanchuma* (Wilna, 1885), Debarim, p. 8a), and these were often repeated by later Jewish and Christian writers. G. F. Moore, 'Biblical notes. 3. The image of Molech', *JBL* 16 (1897), 161–5, has shown convincingly that the rabbinic references were in fact indebted to the classical sources.

7 Translation is from C. H. Oldfather (ed.), *Diodorus of Sicily* (Loeb Classical Library, London and Cambridge, Mass., 1950), p. 365, and *ibid.*, vol. 10 (1954), pp. 179, 181.

SILIUS ITALICUS, *PUNICA* IV.765ff. 'The nation which Dido founded when she landed in Libya were accustomed to appease the gods by human sacrifice and to offer up their young children – horrible to tell – upon fiery altars. Each year the lot was cast and the tragedy was repeated, recalling the sacrifices offered to Diana in the kingdom of Thoas.'[8]

PLUTARCH, *DE SUPERSTITIONE* 13. 'Again, would it not have been far better for the Carthaginians to have taken Critias or Diagoras to draw up their law-code at the very beginning, and so not to believe in any divine power or god, rather than to offer such sacrifices as they used to offer to Kronos? These were not in the manner that Empedocles describes in his attack on those who sacrifice living creatures:

Changed in form is the son beloved of his father so pious,
Who on the altar lays him and slays him. What folly!

No, but with full knowledge and understanding they themselves offered up their own children, and those who had no children would buy little ones from poor people and cut their throats as if they were so many lambs or young birds; meanwhile the mother stood by without a tear or moan; but should she utter a single moan or let fall a single tear, she had to forfeit the money, and her child was sacrificed nevertheless; and the whole area before the statue was filled with a loud noise of flutes and drums so that the cries of the wailing should not reach the ears of the people.'[9]

SEXTUS EMPIRICUS, *OUTLINES OF PYRRHONISM* III.208 AND 221

208. 'And with most of us it is sinful to defile an altar of a god with human blood, but the Laconians lash themselves fiercely over the altar of Artemis Orthosia in order that a great stream of blood may flow over the altar of the goddess. Moreover, some sacrifice a human victim to Kronos, just as the Scythians sacrifice strangers to Artemis; whereas we deem that holy places are defiled by the slaying of a man.'

221. 'To Kronos a human victim is sacrificed [at Carthage], although this is regarded by most as an impious act.'[10]

8 Translation is from J. D. Duff (ed.), *Silius Italicus, Punica* (Loeb Classical Library, London and New York, 1934), p. 225.

9 Translation is from F. C. Babbitt (ed.), *Plutarch's Moralia*, vol. 2 (Loeb Classical Library, London and New York, 1928), p. 493.

10 Translation is from R. G. Bury (ed.), *Sextus Empiricus* (Loeb Classical Library, London and Cambridge, Mass., 1955), pp. 467, 473.

PORPHYRY, *DE ABSTINENTIA* II.27. 'From that time down to the present, not only are communal human sacrifices publicly held in Arcadia at the Lycaean festival and to Kronos in Carthage, but around the world, as memorial of the custom, men sprinkle the altars with kindred blood, although their sacred laws debar anyone guilty of murder from the ceremonies by lustration and by proclamation. Later, then, they moved on to exchange their own bodies for the bodies of the other living creatures in their sacrifices.'

ST AUGUSTINE, *DE CIVITATE DEI* VII.19 AND 26.
VII.19. 'I quote Varro's words: "They have said that Saturn was wont to devour his offspring, because seeds return to the place from which they spring . . ." . . . Next he says that the reason why certain peoples, like the Carthaginians, made a practice of sacrificing children to him, and others, like the Gauls, even adults, is because the best of all seeds is mankind.'
VII.26. 'Perhaps we might compare Saturn with her in this utterly obscene kind of cruelty, or even put him ahead of her, for it is said that he mutilated his father. But in the rites of Saturn men, though they had to be slain by the hands of others, did not have to castrate themselves with their own hands. Saturn devoured his children, as the poets tell the story; and the physical philosophers make of the story what they will. As history relates it, he killed them, yet the Carthaginian practice of sacrificing their children to him was not adopted by the Romans.'[11]

OROSIUS, *ADVERSUS PAGANOS* IV.6.3–5. 'But when among other misfortunes they laboured also with pestilence, they made use of homicides as medicines, for they immolated human beings as sacrificial victims and they brought young children to their altars, which aroused the pity even of the enemy. Regarding this kind of sacrifice, nay, rather sacrilege, I do not find anything which should especially be discussed. For if some demons have had the temerity to order rites of this kind, to satisfy the deaths of men by the slaughter of men, it must have been understood that they were employed as workers and helpers of the pestilence, that they themselves might kill those whom the pestilence had not seized, for it is the custom to offer sound and undefiled victims, so that they might not allay the pestilences but prevent them.'[12]

11 Translation is from W. M. Green (ed.), *Saint Augustine: the City of God Against the Pagans*, vol. 2 (Loeb Classical Library, London and Cambridge, Mass, 1963), pp. 439, 441, 443, 469, 471.

12 Translation is from R. J. Deferrari (ed.), *Paulus Orosius. The Seven Books of History Against the Pagans* (Washington, 1964), pp. 129f.

DRACONTIUS, *CARMINA* V.148–50. 'Carthage carried out every year the murder of two aristocrats, sacrificing children to old Saturn; the parents who wailed sadly near the altars were disfigured.'

TERTULLIAN, *APOLOGY* IX.2–4. 'In Africa infants used to be sacrificed to Saturn, and quite openly, down to the proconsulate of Tiberius, who took the priests themselves and on the very trees of their temple, under whose shadow their crimes had been committed, hung them alive like votive offerings on crosses; and the soldiers of my own country are witnesses to it, who served that proconsul in that very task. Yes, and to this day that holy crime persists in secret. Christians are not the only people who defy you; no crime is ever wholly rooted out; nor does any of your gods change his ways. Saturn did not spare his own children; so, where other people's were concerned, he naturally persisted in not sparing them; and their own parents offered them to him, were glad to respond, and fondled their children that they might not be sacrificed in tears. And between murder and sacrifice – oh! the difference is great!'[13]

MINUCIUS FELIX, *OCTAVIUS* XXX.3. 'Such practices of course follow the precedents set by your gods; Saturn did not indeed expose his sons, but devoured them. Not without reason in some parts of Africa infants were sacrificed to him by their parents, and their cries smothered by endearments and kisses for fear of a victim being sacrificed in tears.'[14]

13 Translation is from T. R. Glover and G. H. Rendall (eds.), *Tertullian, Apology, De Spectaculis, Minucius Felix* (Loeb Classical Library, London and Cambridge, Mass., 1960), p. 47.

14 Translation is from *ibid.*, pp. 407, 409.

BIBLIOGRAPHY

Abarbanel, פרוש התורה (photographed copy of Warsaw edn, 1862. 5pts. in 1 vol.)

Acquaro, E. *et al.* 'Tharros – I', *RSF* 3 (1975), 89–119

'Tharros – II', *RSF* 3 (1975), 213–25

'Tharros – III', *RSF* 4 (1976), 197–228

'Tharros – IV', *RSF* 6 (1978), 63–8

'Tharros – V', *RSF* 7 (1979), 49–124

'Tharros – VI', *RSF* 8 (1980), 79–142

'Tharros – VII', *RSF* 9 (1981), 29–119

'Tharros – VIII', *RSF* 10 (1982), 37–127

'Tharros – IX', *RSF* 11 (1983), 49–111

'Tharros – X', *RSF* 12 (1984), 47–101

'Tharros – XI', *RSF* 13 (1985), 11–147

'Tharros – XII', *RSF* 14 (1986), 95–107

'Tharros – XIII', *RSF* 15 (1987), 75–9

Albright, W. F. 'The evolution of the West-Semitic divinity ʿAn-ʿAnat-ʿAttâ', *AJSL* 41 (1925), 73–101

'Are the Ephod and the Teraphim mentioned in Ugaritic literature?', *BASOR* 83 (1941), 39–42

Yahweh and the Gods of Canaan (London, 1968)

Archaeology and the Religion of Israel, 5th edn (Garden City, 1969)

Alt, A. 'Die phönikischen Inschriften von Karatepe', *Die Welt des Orients* 1 (1949), 272–87

Amadasi, M. G. *et al. Monte Sirai*, vols. 2–4 (Rome, 1965–7)

Andersen, F. I. and Freedman, D. N. *Hosea* (Garden City, 1980)

Arnold, W. R. *Ephod and Ark* (Cambridge, Mass., 1917)

Astour, M. C. 'Sepharvaim', *The Interpreter's Dictionary of the Bible Supplementary Volume* (Nashville, 1976), p. 807

Babbitt, F. C. *et al. Plutarch's Moralia* (15 vols., Loeb Classical Library, London, New York etc., 1927–69)

Baentsch, B. *Exodus-Leviticus-Numeri* (Göttingen, 1903)

Baethgen, F. *Beiträge zur semitischen Religionsgeschichte* (Berlin, 1888)

Bailey, L. R. 'Gehenna', *The Interpreter's Dictionary of the Bible Supplementary Volume* (Nashville, 1976), pp. 353–4

Bardy, G. and Sender, J. (eds.) *Théophile d'Antioche. Trois Livres à Autolycus* (Sources chrétiens, Paris, 1948)

Barreca, F. and Garbini, G. *Monte Sirai*, vol. 1 (Rome, 1964)

Barreca, F. and Bondi. S. F. 'Scavi nel *tofet* di Monte Sirai, campagna 1979', *RSF* 8 (1980), 143–5

Barth, J. ' שׁוֹט שֹׁטֵף ', *ZAW* 33 (1913), 306–7

'Zu שׁוֹט "Flut" ', *ZAW* 34 (1914), 69

Bartolini, P. and Bondi, S. F. 'Monte Sirai 1980', *RSF*, 9 (1981), 216–30

Bartolini, P. and Tronchetti, C. *La necropoli di Nora* (Rome, 1981)

Baudissin, W. W. F. Graf von *Jahve et Moloch* (Leipzig, 1874)

'Baal und Bel' in A. Hauck (ed.), *Realencyklopädie für protestantische Theologie und Kirche*, vol. 2, 3rd edn (Leipzig, 1897), pp. 323–40.

'Moloch', in A. Hauck (ed.), *Realencyklopädie für protestantische Theologie und Kirche*, vol. 13, 3rd edn (Leipzig, 1903), pp. 269–303

Bea, A. 'Kinderopfer für Moloch oder für Jahwe?', *Biblica* 18 (1937), 95–107

Bennett, W. H. 'Molech, Moloch' in J. Hastings (ed.), *A Dictionary of the Bible*, vol. 3 (Edinburgh, 1900), pp. 415–17

Bentzen, A. *Jesaja* (2 vols. in 1, Copenhagen, 1943–4)

Berthier, A. and Charlier, R. *Le Sanctuaire Punique d'El-Hofra à Constantine* (Paris, 1955)

Bochart, S. *Phaleg et Canaan* (Leiden, 1707)

Boettcher, F. *De inferis*, vol. 1 (Dresden, 1846)

Boling, R. G. *Judges* (Garden City, 1975)

Bonar, H. 'Topheth' in W. Smith (ed.), *A Dictionary of the Bible*, vol. 3 (London, 1863), pp. 1563–4

Bonnet, C. *Melqart* (Studia Phoenicia 8, Louvain, 1988)

Borger, R. 'Amos 5,26, Apostelgeschichte 7, 43 und Šurpu II, 180', *ZAW* 100 (1988), 70–81

Bottéro, J. and Finet, A. (eds.) *Archives Royales de Mari*, vol. 15 (Paris, 1954)

Box, G. H. *The Book of Isaiah* (London, 1908)

Braun, J. *Selecta sacra* (Amsterdam, 1700)

Bright, J. *Jeremiah*, 2nd edn (Garden City, 1978)

Brockelmann, C. *Lexicon Syriacum*, 2nd edn (Halle, 1928)

Brown, F., Driver, S. R., and Briggs, C. A. *A Hebrew and English Lexicon of the Old Testament* (Oxford, 1907; reprinted with corrections, 1953)

Buber, M. *Königtum Gottes*, 3rd edn (Heidelberg, 1956). ET, *Kingship of God* (London, 1967)

Buber, S. (ed.) *Midrasch Tanchuma* (Wilna, 1885)

Buccellati, G. *The Amorites of the Ur III Period* (Naples, 1966)

Burney, C. F. *The Book of Judges* (London, 1920)

Bury, R. G. (ed.) *Sextus Empiricus* (Loeb Classical Library, London and Cambridge, Mass., 1955)

Carcopino, J. 'Survivances par substitution des sacrifices d'enfants dans l'Afrique romaine', *RHR* 105 (1932), 592–9
Carroll, R. P. *From Chaos to Covenant* (London, 1981)
Cassuto, U. (M.D.) האלה ענת (Jerusalem, 1951). ET, *The Goddess Anath* (Jerusalem, 1971)
Cazelles, H. 'The problem of the kings in Osee, 8:4', *CBQ* 11 (1949), 14–25
'Molok' in L. Pirot, A. Robert and H. Cazelles (eds.), *Dictionnaire de la Bible Supplément*, vol. 5 (Paris, 1957), cols. 1337–46
'David's monarchy and the Gibeonite claim', *PEQ* 87 (1955), 165–75
Cecchini, S. 'Les stèles du tophet de Sulcis' in *Actes du deuxième Congrès International d'études des Cultures de la Méditerranée Occidentale* (Algiers, 1978), pp. 90–108
Chabot, J.-B. 'Note complémentaire de M. J.-B. Chabot', *CRAIBL* (1931), 26–7
Charles, R. H. 'Gehenna' in J. Hastings (ed.), *A Dictionary of the Bible*, vol. 2 (Edinburgh, 1899), pp. 119–20
Charles-Picard, G. *Les Religions de l'Afrique antique* (Paris, 1954)
Charlier, R. 'La nouvelle série de stèles puniques de Constantine et la question des sacrifices dits "molchomor", en relation avec l'expression "BŠRM BTM"', *Karthago* 4 (1953), 1–48
Cheyne, T. K. *The Prophecies of Isaiah*, 2nd edn (2 vols., London, 1882)
Chiera, G. *Testmonianze su Nora* (Collezione di studi fenici 11, Rome, 1978)
Ciasca A. 'Mozia (Sicilia): il *tofet*. Campagne 1971–72', *RSF* 1 (1973), 94–8
Ciasca A. *et al. Mozia*, vols 1–9 (Rome, 1964–78)
Clements, R. E. *Isaiah 1–39* (London, 1980)
Cogan, M. *Imperialism and Religion* (Missoula, 1974)
Cook, A. B. *Zeus* (3 vols. in 5, London, 1914–40)
Cooper, A. 'Divine names and epithets in the Ugaritic texts' in S. Rummel (ed.), *Ras Shamra Parallels*, vol. 3 (Rome, 1981) pp. 333–469
Corpus Inscriptionum Latinarum (Berlin, 1863–)
Corpus Inscriptionum Semiticarum (Paris, 1881–)
Cross, F. M. *Canaanite Myth and Hebrew Epic* (Cambridge, Mass., 1973)
Curtis, J. B. 'An investigation of the Mount of Olives in the Judaeo-Christian tradition', *HUCA* 28 (1957), 137–77
Dahood, M. *Ugaritic–Hebrew Philology* (Rome, 1965)
Daumer, G. F. *Der Feuer- und Molochdienst der alten Hebräer* (Braunschweig, 1842)
Davies, P. R. 'Ark or ephod in 1 Sam. XIV. 18?', *JTS* 26, NS (1975), 82–7
Day, J. *God's Conflict with the Dragon and the Sea: Echoes of a Canaanite Myth in the Old Testament* (Cambridge, 1985)
Deferrari, R. J. (ed.) *Paulus Orosius. The Seven Books of History Against the Pagans* (Washington, 1964)
Delitzsch, F. *Wo lag das Paradies?* (Leipzig, 1881)
Deller, K. Review of R. de Vaux, *Les Sacrifices de l'Ancien Testament*, *Orientalia* 34, NS (1965), 382–6

Derchain, P. 'Les plus anciens témoignages de sacrifices d'enfants chez les Sémites occidentaux', *VT*, 20 (1970), 351–5
Dhorme, E. *Les Livres de Samuel* (Paris, 1910)
'Le dieu Baal et le dieu Moloch dans la tradition biblique', *Anatolian Studies* 6 (1956), 57–61
Le Livre de Job (Paris, 1926). ET, *A Commentary on the Book of Job* (London, 1967; reprinted Nashville, 1984)
Dietrich, M., Loretz, O., and Sanmartín, J. *Die keilalphabetischen Texte aus Ugarit. Teil 1: Transkription* (*AOAT* 24, Neukirchen-Vluyn, 1976)
Dietzsch, D. 'De cultu Molochi' in B. Ugolini (ed.), *Thesaurus Antiquitatum Sacrarum*, vol. 23 (Venice, 1760), pp. 861–86
Donner, H. *Israel unter den Völkern* (*SVT* 11, 1964)
Donner, H. and Röllig, W. *Kanaanäische und aramäische Inschriften* (3 vols., Wiesbaden, 1966–9)
Dossin, G. 'Signaux lumineux au pays de Mari', *RA* 35 (1938), 174–86
Driver, G. R. 'Studies in the vocabulary of the Old Testament. II', *JTS* 32 (1931), 250–7
'Studies in the vocabulary of the Old Testament. V', *JTS* 34 (1934), 33–44
'Studies in the vocabulary of the Old Testament. VII', *JTS* 35 (1934), 380–93
'Difficult words in the Hebrew prophets' in H. H. Rowley (ed.), *Studies in Old Testament Prophecy Presented to Professor Theodore H. Robinson* (Edinburgh, 1950), pp. 52–72
'Geographical problems', *Eretz-Israel* 5 (Jerusalem, 1958), 16*–20*
' "Another little drink" – Isaiah 28:1–22' in P. R. Ackroyd and B. Lindars (eds.), *Words and Meanings. Essays Presented to David Winton Thomas* (Cambridge, 1968), 47–67
Review of A. Phillips, *Ancient Israel's Criminal Law*, *JTS* 23, NS (1972), 160–4
Driver, S. R. *Notes on the Hebrew Text of the Books of Samuel* (Oxford, 1890)
The Books of Joel and Amos, 2nd edn (Cambridge, 1915)
Dronkert, K. *De Molochdienst in het Oude Testament* (Leiden, 1953)
Het Mensenoffer in de Ou–Testamentische wereld (Baarn, 1955)
Duff, J. D. (ed.) *Silius Italicus, Punica* (Loeb Classical Library, London and New York, 1934)
Duhm, B. *Das Buch Jesaja*, 4th edn (Göttingen, 1922)
Dunand, M. *Fouilles de Byblos* (5 vols. in 8, Paris, 1939–73)
Dussaud, R. Review of O. Eissfeldt, *Molk als Opferbegriff, Syria* 16 (1935), 407–9
Review of O. Eissfeldt, *Molk als Opferbegriff*, *Archiv für Orientforschung* 11 (1936), 167f
Les Origines cananéennes du sacrifice israélite, 2nd edn (Paris, 1941)
'Précisions épigraphiques touchant les sacrifices puniques d'enfants', *CRAIBL* (1946), 371–87
Ebach, J. and Rüterswörden, U. 'ADRMLK "Moloch" und BAʿAL ADR', *UF* 11 (1979), 219–26

Ebeling, E. *Tod und Leben nach den Vorstellungen der Babylonier. 1. Texte* (Berlin and Leipzig, 1931)
Eerdmans, B. D. *Melekdienst en Vereering van Hemellichamen in Israël's Assyrische Periode* (Leiden, 1891)
Eichrodt, W. *Theologie des Alten Testaments*, 5th edn (3 vols., Leipzig, 1957–65). ET, *Theology of the Old Testament* (2 vols., London, 1961–7)
Der Prophet Hesekiel (2 vols., Göttingen, 1959–66). ET, *Ezekiel* (London, 1970)
Eissfeldt, O. *Molk als Opferbegriff im Punischen und Hebräischen und das Ende des Gottes Moloch* (Halle, 1935)
'The beginnings of Phoenician epigraphy according to a letter written by Wilhelm Gesenius in 1835', *PEQ* 79 (1947), 68–86
'Adrammelek und Demarus', *Annuaire de l'Institut de Philologie et d'Histoire Orientales et Slaves* 13 (1953, but published 1955), 153–9; reprinted in *Kleine Schriften zum Alten Testament*, vol. 3 (Tübingen, 1966), pp. 335–9
Ellermeier, F. 'Das Verbum חוש in Koh 2 25', *ZAW* 75, NS 34 (1963), 197–217
Elliger, K. 'Der Sinn des Wortes Chammân', *ZDPV* 66 (1943), 129–39
'Das Gesetz Leviticus 18', *ZAW* 67 (1955), 1–25; reprinted in *Kleine Schriften zum Alten Testament* (Munich, 1966), pp. 232–59
'Ephod und Choschen', *VT* 8 (1958), 19–35
Epstein, I. (ed.) *The Babylonian Talmud* (35 vols., London, 1935–52)
Fedele, F. 'Anthropologia fisica e paleocologia di Tharros: Nota preliminare sugli scavi del *tofet*, campagna 1976', *RSF* 5 (1977), 185–93
Ferrara, A. J., and Parker, S. B. 'Seating arrangements at divine banquets', *UF* 4 (1972), 37–9
Février, J.-G. 'À propos de Ba'al Addir', *Semitica* 2 (1949), 21–8
'Molchomor', *RHR* 143 (1953), 8–18
'Essai de reconstruction du sacrifice molek', *JA* 248 (1960), 167–87
Fey, R. *Amos und Jesaja* (*WMANT* 12, Neukirchen-Vluyn, 1963)
Field, F. *Origenis Hexaplorum quae supersunt* (2 vols., Oxford, 1875)
Finkelstein, L. *Siphre ad Deuteronomium; H. S. Horovitzii schedis usus cum variis lectionibus et adnotationibus* (Berlin, 1939; reprinted New York, 1969)
Fohrer, G. *Das Buch Jesaja* (3 vols., Zurich and Stuttgart, 1960–4)
Foote, T. C. 'The ephod', *JBL* 21 (1902), 1–47
Fraenkel, S. *Die aramäischen Fremdwörter im Arabischen* (Leiden, 1886)
Frankena, R. *Tākultu, de sacrale maaltijd in het Assyrische ritueel* (Leiden, 1953)
Friedrich, J., Meyer, G. R., Ungnad, A., and Weidner, E. F. *Die Inschriften vom Tell Halaf* (*Archiv für Orientforschung Beiheft* 6, Berlin, 1940)
Friedrich, J. and Röllig, W. *Phönizisch–Punische Grammatik*, 2nd edn (Rome, 1970)

Gabriel, J. *Untersuchungen über das alttestamentliche Priestertum, mit besonderer Berücksichtigung des hohenpriesterlichen Ornates* (Vienna, 1933)

Galling, K. 'Baʿal Ḥammon in Kition und die ḥammanîm' in H. Gese and H. P. Rüger (eds.), *Wort und Geschichte. Festschrift für Karl Elliger zum 70. Geburtstag* (*AOAT* 18, Neukirchen-Vluyn, 1973), pp. 65–70

Gaster, T. H. *Myth, Legend, and Custom in the Old Testament* (London, 1969)

Geiger, A. *Urschrift und Uebersetzungen der Bibel* (Breslau, 1857)

'Der Baal in den hebräischen Eigennamen', *ZDMG* 16 (1862), 728–32

Gelb, I. J. *Computer-aided Analysis of Amorite* (Chicago, 1980)

Gelston, A. 'Kingship in the book of Hosea', *OTS* 19 (1974), 71–85

Gese, H. 'Die strömende Geissel des Hadad und Jesaja 28, 15 und 18' in A. Kuschke and E. Kutsch (eds.), *Archäologie und Altes Testament* (Festschrift für Kurt Galling, Tübingen, 1970), pp. 127–34

'Ezechiel 20, 25f. und die Erstgeburtsopfer' in H. Donner, R. Hanhart and R. Smend (eds.), *Beiträge zur Alttestamentlichen Theologie* (Festschrift für Walther Zimmerli zum 70. Geburtstag, Göttingen, 1977), pp. 140–51

Gesenius, W. *Thesaurus philologicus criticus linguae Hebraeae et Chaldaeae Veteris Testamenti* (Leipzig, 1829–58)

Gevirtz, S. 'A new look at an old crux: Amos 5 26', *JBL* 87 (1968), 267–76

Ghillany, F. W. (=von der Alm, R.) *Die Menschenopfer der alten Hebräer* (Nürnberg, 1842)

Gibson, J. C. L. *Textbook of Syrian Semitic Inscriptions* (3 vols., Oxford, 1971–82)

Gifford, E. H. *Eusebii Pamphili evangelicae praeparationis* (4 vols. in 5, Oxford, 1903)

Glover, T. R. and Rendall, G. H. (eds.), *Tertullian, Apology, De Spectaculis, Minucius Felix* (Loeb Classical Library, London and Cambridge, Mass., 1960)

Godwin, T. *Moses and Aaron* (London, 1625)

Gordis, R. *The Book of Job* (New York, 1978)

Gordon, C. H. *Ugaritic Textbook* (3 vols., Rome, 1965)

'"In" of predication or equivalence', *JBL* 100 (1981), 612–13

Gray, J. 'The desert god ʿAṯtr in the literature and religion of Canaan', *JNES* 8 (1949), 72–83

The Legacy of Canaan, 2nd edn, *SVT* 5 (1965)

I & II Kings, 3rd edn (London, 1977)

Green, A. R. W. *The Role of Human Sacrifice in the Ancient Near East* (*ASOR* Dissertation Series 1, Missoula, 1975)

Green, W. M. (ed.) *Saint Augustine: the City of God against the Pagans*, vol. 2 (Loeb Classical Library, London and Cambridge, Mass., 1963)

Greenfield, J. C. 'The prepositions b..... taḥat in Jes 57 5', *ZAW* 73 (1961), 226–8

Griffiths, J. G. *Plutarch's De Iside et Osiride* (Cardiff, 1970)
Gröndahl, F. *Die Personennamen der Texte aus Ugarit* (Rome, 1967)
Guillaume, A. 'Isaiah's oracle against Assyria (Isaiah 30, 27–33) in the light of archaeology', *BSOAS* 17 (1955), 413–15
Haag, H. (ed.) 'Tophet' in *Bibel-Lexikon*, 2nd edn (Einsiedeln, Zurich and Cologne, 1968) col. 1766
Hammershaimb, E. *The Book of Amos. A Commentary* (ET, Oxford, 1970)
Haran, M. ' צורת האפוד במקורות המקראיים ', *Tarbiz* 24 (1955), 380–91 (English summary on pp. II–III)
Harden, D. *The Phoenicians* (London, 1962)
Harper, W. R. *A Critical and Exegetical Commentary on Amos and Hosea* (Edinburgh, 1905)
Harrelson, W. J. 'Molech, Moloch' in H. H. Rowley and F. C. Grant (eds.), *Dictionary of the Bible*, 2nd edn of the work originally edited by J. Hastings (Edinburgh, 1963), 669
Healey, J. F., '*Malkū: mlkm: Anunnaki*', *UF* 7 (1975), 235–8
'*MLKM/RPʾUM* and the *KISPUM*', *UF* 10 (1979), 89–91
Heider, G. C. *The Cult of Molek: A Reassessment* (Sheffield, 1985, but actually appeared in 1986)
Herbert, A. S. *The Book of the Prophet Isaiah* (Cambridge, 1973)
Herdner, A. *Corpus des tablettes en cunéiformes alphabétiques* (2 vols., Paris, 1963)
'Une prière à Baal des ugaritiens en danger', *CRAIBL* (1972), 693–703
'Nouveaux textes alphabétiques de Ras Shamra – XXIVe campagne, 1961', in C. F. A. Schaeffer (ed.), *Ugaritica* VII (Paris, 1978), 1–74
Herr, L. G. *The Scripts of Ancient Northwest Semitic Seals* (Missoula, 1978)
Hill, G. F. *Catalogue of the Greek Coins of Phoenicia* (London, 1910)
Hoffmann, G. 'Lexikalisches', *ZAW* 2 (1882), 53–72
Hoftijzer, J. 'Eine Notiz zum punischen Kinderopfer', *VT* 8 (1958), 288–92
Hoonacker, A. van *Le Voeu de Jephté. Etude sur le chapitre XI du livre des Juges, suivie d'une notice sur Ezéchiel XX 25–26* (Louvain, 1893)
Les Douze Petits Prophètes (Paris, 1908)
Huber, F. *Jahwe, Juda und die anderen Völker beim Propheten Jesaja* (*BZAW* 137, 1976)
Huffmon, H. B. *Amorite Personal Names in the Mari Texts* (Baltimore, 1965)
Hvidberg-Hansen, F. O. *La Déesse TNT* (2 vols., Copenhagen, 1979)
Ingholt, H. 'Le sens du mot Hammān' in *Mélanges Syriens offerts à Monsieur René Dussaud*, vol. 2 (Paris, 1939), pp. 795–802
Irsigler, H. *Gottesgericht und Jahwetag* (St Ottilien, 1977)
Irwin, W. H. *Isaiah 28–33. Translation with Philological Notes* (Rome, 1977)
Isbell, C. D. 'Another look at Amos 5:26', *JBL* 97 (1978), 97–9
Israel, F. 'The language of the Ammonites', *Orientalia Lovaniensia Periodica* 10 (1979), 143–59
Jackson, K. P. *The Ammonite Language of the Iron Age* (Chico, 1983)
Janzen, J. G. *Studies in the Text of Jeremiah* (Cambridge, Mass., 1973)

Jastrow, M. *A Dictionary of the Targumim, the Talmud Babli and Yerushalmi, and the Midrashic Literature* (2 vols., New York, 1950)

Jensen, P., Review of H. V. Hilprecht, *The Babylonian Expedition of the University of Pennsylvania, Zeitschrift für Assyriologie*, 13 (1898), 329–36

'Alttestamentlich-Keilschriftliches. II. Die Götter כְּמוֹשׁ und מֶלֶךְ und die Erscheinungsformen *Kammuš* und *Malik* des assyrisch-babylonischen Gottes *Nergal*', *Zeitschrift für Assyriologie* 42, NS 8 (1934), 235–7

Jeremias, J., ' γέεννα ' in G. Kittel (ed.), *Theologisches Wörterbuch zum Neuen Testament*, vol. 1 (Stuttgart, 1933), pp. 655–6. ET, *Theological Dictionary of the New Testament*, vol. 1 (Grand Rapids and London, 1964), pp. 657–8

Jirku, A. 'Gab es im Alten Testament einen Gott Molek (Melek)?', *Archiv für Religionswissenschaft* 35 (1938), 178–9

Johns, C. H. W. *Assyrian Deeds and Documents* (4 vols., Cambridge, 1898–1923)

Johnson, A. R. *Sacral Kingship in Ancient Israel*, 2nd edn (Cardiff, 1967)

Jones, G. H. *1 and 2 Kings* (2 vols., London and Grand Rapids, 1984)

Kaiser, O. *Der Prophet Jesaja Kapitel 13–39* (Göttingen, 1973). ET, *Isaiah 13–39* (London, 1974)

'Den Erstgeborenen deiner Söhne sollst du mir geben,' O. Kaiser (ed.), *Denkender Glaube. Festschrift C. H. Ratschow* (Berlin and New York, 1976)

Kamphausen, A. H. H. *Das Verhältnis des Menschenopfers zur israelitischen Religion* (Bonn, 1896)

Kapelrud, A. S. 'King and fertility. A discussion of II Sam 21:1–14' in *Interpretationes ad Vetus Testamentum pertinentes Sigmundo Mowinckel septuagenario missae* (Oslo, 1955), pp. 113–22

The Message of the Prophet Zephaniah (Oslo, Bergen and Tromsø, 1975)

Karageorghis, V. *Cyprus* (London, 1982)

Kaufman, S. A. 'An Assyro-Aramaic *egirtu ša šulmu*' in M. de Jong Ellis (ed.), *Essays on the Ancient Near East in Memory of Jacob Joel Finkelstein* (Hamden, 1977), pp. 119–27

'The enigmatic Adad-milki', *JNES* 37 (1978), 101–9

Keel, O. 'Kanaanäische Sühneriten auf ägyptischen Tempelsreliefs', *VT* 25 (1975), 413–69

Keil, C. F. *Biblische Commentar über die prophetischen Geschichtsbücher des Alten Testaments* (Leipzig, 1875)

Kelsey, F. W. *Excavations at Carthage, 1925: A Preliminary Report* (New York, 1926)

Kirkpatrick, A. F. *The Second Book of Samuel* (Cambridge, 1899)

Kittel, R. *Geschichte des Volkes Israel*, 5th and 6th edns (2 vols., Gotha, 1923–5)

Klopfenstein, M. A. *Die Lüge nach dem Alten Testament* (Zurich and Frankfurt, 1964)

Koehler, L. and Baumgartner, W. *Lexicon in Veteris Testamenti Libros* (Leiden, 1958)

Kohler, J. and Ungnad, A. *Assyrische Rechtsurkunden* (Leipzig, 1913)

König, E. *Das Buch Jesaia* (Gütersloh, 1926)

Kornfeld, W. 'Der Moloch. Eine Untersuchung zur Theorie O. Eissfeldts', *Wiener Zeitschrift für die Kunde des Morgenlandes* 51 (1952), 287–313

'Moloch' in H. Haag (ed.), *Bibel-Lexikon* (Einsiedeln, Zurich and Cologne, 1968), cols. 1163–4

Kuenen, A. 'Critische bijdragen tot de geschiedenis van den Israëlietischen godsdienst. I. De integriteit van Ex. XIII:11–16', *Theologisch Tijdschrift* 1 (1867), 53–72

'Critische bijdragen tot de geschiedenis van den Israëlietischen godsdienst. III. Jahveh en Moloch', *Theologisch Tijdschrift* 2 (1868), 559–98

De Godsdienst van Israël (2 vols., Haarlem, 1869–70). ET, *The Religion of Israel* (3 vols., London, 1874–5)

Lagrange, M.-J. *Etudes sur les religions sémitiques*, 2nd edn (Paris, 1905)

Lambert, W. G. 'Götterlisten', E. Weidner and W. von Soden (eds.), *Reallexikon der Assyriologie*, vol. 3 (Berlin and New York, 1957–71), pp. 473–9

Landsberger, B. *Sam'al* (Ankara, 1948)

Langdon, S. (ed.) *The H. Weld-Blundell Collection in the Ashmolean Museum. 1. Sumerian and Semitic Religious and Historical Texts*, Oxford edns of cuneiform texts, vol. 1 (Oxford, 1923)

Leglay, A. *Saturne Africain. Monuments* (2 vols., Paris, 1961–6)

Saturne Africain. Histoire (Paris, 1966)

Lehmann, M. 'A new interpretation of the term שדמות', *VT* 3 (1953), 361–71

Levi della Vida, G. 'Some notes on the stele of Ben-Hadad', *BASOR* 90 (1943), 30–4

Lévy, I. 'Malcandre dans l'inscription d'Eschmounazar', *Revue archéologique* 4 (1904), 385–99

Lidzbarski, M. 'Neue Götter', *Nachrichten von der königlichen Gesellschaft der Wissenschaften zu Göttingen* (Phil.-hist. Klasse, Heft 1, Göttingen, 1916)

Lindblom, J. 'Der Eckstein in Jes. 28, 16' in *Interpretationes ad Vetus Testamentum pertinentes Sigmundo Mowinckel septuagenario missae* (Oslo, 1955), pp. 123–32

'Lot-casting in the Old Testament', *VT* 12 (1962), 164–78

Lipiński, E. 'La Fête de l'ensevelissement et la résurrection de Melqart', *Actes de la XVIIe Rencontre Assyriologique Internationale* (Ham-sur-Heure, 1970), 30–58

Mader, E. *Die Menschenopfer der alten Hebräer und der benachbarten Völker* (Freiburg, 1909)

Marcus, D. *Jephthah and His Vow* (Lubbock, 1986)

Margalit, B. '(RS 24.266) תפילה אוגריתית לעת מצור', *Proceedings of the Seventh World Congress of Jewish Studies. Studies in the Bible and the*

Ancient Near East (Jerusalem, 1981), 63–83 (Hebrew section)
'Why King Mesha of Moab sacrificed his oldest son', *BARev* 12, no. 6 (Nov./Dec., 1986), 62–3, 76
Margulis, B. (= Margalit, B.) 'A Ugaritic Psalm (RŠ 24.252)', *JBL* 89 (1970), 292–304
Mauchline, J. *Isaiah 1–39* (London, 1962)
May, H. G. 'Ephod and Ariel', *AJSL* 56 (1939), 44–52
Mayer, M. 'Kronos' in W. H. Roscher (ed.), *Ausführliches Lexikon der griechischen und römischen Mythologie*, vol. 2 (Leipzig, 1890–7), cols. 1452–1573
Mays, J. L. *Amos* (London, 1969)
Hosea (London, 1969)
McCarter, P. K. *II Samuel* (Garden City, 1984)
McKane, W. 'Jeremiah II 23–25: observations on the versions and history of exegesis', *OTS* 17 (1972), 73–88
Meier, E. Reviews of G. F. Daumer, *Der Feuer- und Molochdienst der alten Hebräer*, and F. W. Ghillany (= R. von der Alm), *Die Menschenopfer der alten Hebräer*, *Theologische Studien und Kritiken* 16 (1843), 1007–1053
Meissner, B. 'Die Keilschrifttexte auf den steinernen Orthostaten und Statuen aus dem Tell Ḥalâf', *Aus fünf Jahrtausenden morgenländischer Kultur. Festschrift Max Freiherrn von Oppenheim zum 70. Geburtstage* (*Archiv für Orientforschung Beiheft* 1, Berlin, 1933), pp. 71–9
Menzel, B. *Assyrische Tempel* (2 vols., Rome, 1981)
Migne, J. P. (ed.) 'S. Eusebii Hieronymi Stridonensis Presbyteri Commentariorum in Jeremiam prophetam libri sex' in *Patrologiae cursus completus, Series Latina*, vol. 24 (Paris, 1865), cols. 679–900
Milik, J. T. 'An unpublished arrow-head with Phoenician inscription of the 11th–10th century B.C.', *BASOR* 143 (1956), 3–6
Miller, I. D. 'Other gods and idols in the period of Hosea' (Unpublished M. Litt. thesis, Cambridge, 1975)
Miller, J. M., 'Jebus and Jerusalem: a case of mistaken identity', *ZDPV* 90 (1974), 115–27
Miqraoth Gedoloth (5 vols., Warsaw, 1874)
Mommert, C. *Menschenopfer bei den alten Hebräern* (Leipzig, 1905)
Montgomery, J. A. 'The holy city and Gehenna', *JBL* 27 (1908), 24–47
Montgomery, J. A. and Gehman, H. S. *A Critical and Exegetical Commentary on the Books of Kings* (Edinburgh, 1951)
Moore, G. F. *A Critical and Exegetical Commentary on Judges* (Edinburgh, 1895)
'Biblical notes. 3. The image of Molech', *JBL* 16 (1897), 161–5
'Milcom' in *Encyclopaedia Biblica*, vol. 3 (London, 1902), cols. 3085–6
'Molech, Moloch' in *Encyclopaedia Biblica*, vol. 3 (London, 1902), cols. 3183–91
Morgenstern, J. 'The Ark, the Ephod and the Tent of Meeting', *HUCA* 18 (1943–4), 1–17

Mosca, P. G. 'Child sacrifice in Canaanite and Israelite religion: A study in Mulk and Molech' (unpublished Ph.D thesis, Harvard University, 1975)

Moscati, S. 'Il sacrificio dei fanciulli', *Rendiconti della Pontificia Accademia Romana di Archeologia* 38 (1965–6), 61–8

The World of the Phoenicians (ET, London, 1968)

'New light on Punic art' in W. A. Ward (ed.), *The Role of the Phoenicians in the Interaction of Mediterranean Civilizations* (Beirut, 1968), 65–75

Movers, F. C. *Die Phönizier* (3 vols. in 4, Bonn, 1841–56)

Mulder, M. J. *Kanaänitische goden in het Oude Testament* (The Hague, 1965)

Müller, A. *Glossarium Sacrum* (Frankfurt, 1690)

Müller, K. F. *Das assyrische Ritual: 1. Texte zum assyrischen Königsritual* (Leipzig, 1937)

Münter, F. C. C. H. *Religion der Karthager*, 2nd edn (Copenhagen, 1821)

Noth, M. *Das dritte Buch Mose, Leviticus* (Göttingen, 1962). ET, *Leviticus* (London, 1965)

Nyberg, H. S. *Studien zum Hoseabuche* (Uppsala, 1935)

O'Ceallaigh, G. C. ' "And *so* David did to *all the cities* of Ammon" ', *VT* 12 (1962), 179–89

Oldfather, C. H. *et al.* (eds.) *Diodorus of Sicily* (12 vols., Loeb Classical Library, London and Cambridge, Mass., 1933–67)

Oort, H. *Het menschenoffer in Israël* (Haarlem, 1865)

Oppenheim, A. L. 'Assyriological gleanings', *BASOR* 107 (1947), 7–11

Östborn, G. *Yahweh and Baal: Studies in the Book of Hosea and Related Documents* (Lund, 1956)

Pardee, D. 'The preposition in Ugaritic', *UF* 8 (1976), 215–322

'Letters from Tel Arad', *UF* 10 (1978), 289–336

'A philological and prosodic analysis of the Ugaritic serpent incantation *UT* 607', *JANESCU* 10 (1978), 73–108

Parpola, S. 'The murderer of Sennacherib' in B. Alster (ed.), *Mesopotamia 8. Death in Mesopotamia. Papers Read at the XXVIe Rencontre Assyriologique Internationale* (Copenhagen, 1980), 171–82

Penna, A. *Isaia* (Turin and Rome, 1964)

Perrot, G. and Chipiez, C. *Histoire de l'art*, vol. 3 (Paris, 1885)

Pesce, G. *Sardegna punica* (Cagliari, 1961)

Phillips, A. 'David's linen ephod', *VT* 19 (1969), 485–7

Ancient Israel's Criminal Law (Oxford, 1970)

Plataroti, D. 'Zum Gebrauch des Wortes *mlk* im Alten Testament', *VT* 28 (1978), 286–300

Pohl, A. 'Miszellen', *Biblica* 22 (1941), 35–7

Pohlenz, M. 'Kronos' in G. Wissowa and W. Kroll (eds.), *Paulys Real-Encyclopädie der classischen Altertumswissenschaft*, vol. 11 (Stuttgart, 1922), cols. 1982–2018

Poinssot, L. and Lantier, R. 'Un sanctuaire de Tanit à Carthage', *RHR* 44 (1923), 32–68

Pope, M. H. *Job*, 3rd edn. (Garden City, 1973)
'Notes on the Ugaritic Rephaim Texts' in M. de Jong Ellis (ed.), *Essays on the Ancient Near East in Memory of Jacob Joel Finkelstein* (Hamden, 1977), pp. 163–82
Power, E. 'Isaias (Isaiah)' in B. Orchard, E. F. Sutcliffe, R. C. Fuller, R. Russell (eds.), *A Catholic Commentary on Holy Scripture* (London, 1953), 539–73
Poznański, S. 'Zu שׁוֹט שֹׁטֵף ', *ZAW* 36 (1916), 119–20
Preuss, H. D. *Verspottung fremder Religionen im Alten Testament* (*BWANT* 92, Stuttgart, 1971)
Priebatsch, H. Y. 'Jerusalem und die Brunnenstrasse Merneptahs', *ZDPV* 9 (1975), 18–29
Pritchard, J. B. (ed.) *Ancient Near Eastern Texts Relating to the Old Testament*, 3rd edn (Princeton, 1969)
Recovering Sarepta, a Phoenician City (Princeton, 1978)
Procksch, O. *Jesaia*, vol. 1 (Leipzig, 1930)
Rahlfs, A. *Septuaginta, id est Vetus Testamentum Graece iuxta LXX interpres* (2 vols., Stuttgart, 1935)
Raoul-Rochette, D. *Mémoires d'archéologie comparée, asiatique, grecque et étrusque. Premier Mémoire sur l'Hercule assyrien et phénicien, considéré dans ses rapports avec l'Hercule grec* (Paris, 1848)
Reiner, E. *Šurpu. A Collection of Sumerian and Akkadian Incantations* (*Archiv für Orientforschung Beiheft* 11, 1958)
Ribichini, S. 'Un 'ipotesi per Milkʿaštart', *RSO* 50 (1976), 43–55
Riehm, E. C. A. (ed.) *Handwörterbuch des Biblischen Altertums* (2 vols., Bielefeld and Leipzig, 1884)
Robinson, E. *Biblical Researches in Palestine* (3 vols., London, 1841; 3rd edn, 1867)
Robinson, T. H. and Horst, F. *Die zwölf kleinen Propheten* (Tübingen, 1954)
Rolfe, J. C. (ed.) *Quintus Curtius* (Loeb Classical Library, London and Cambridge, Mass., 1946)
Rosenmüller, E. F. C. *Scholia in Vetus Testamentum. Partis octavae, Ieremiae vaticinia et Threnos continentis, volumen primum* (Leipzig, 1826)
Rosensohn Jacobs, V. and I. 'The myth of Môt and 'Al'eyan Baʿal', *HTR* 38 (1945) 77–109
Rowley, H. H. Review of K. Dronkert, *De Molochdienst in het Oude Testament*, *Bibliotheca Orientalis* 10 (1953), cols. 195–6
Dictionary of Bible Themes (London, 1968)
Job (London, 1970)
Rudolph, W. *Hosea* (Gütersloh, 1966)
Jeremia, 3rd edn (Tübingen, 1968)
Rummel, S. (ed.) *Ras Shamra Parallels*, vol. 3 (Rome, 1981)
Sabottka, L. *Zephanja. Versuch einer Neuübersetzung mit philologischem Kommentar* (Rome, 1972)
Sale, G. (ed.) *The Koran* (London and New York, 1890)

Salmond, S. D. F. 'Tophet, Topheth' in J. Hastings (ed.), *A Dictionary of the Bible*, vol. 4 (Edinburgh, 1902), pp. 797–9

Šanda, A. *Die Bücher der Könige* (2 vols., Münster, 1911–12)

Sarna, N. M. 'The mythological background of Job 18', *JBL* 82 (1963), 315–18

Sawyer, J. F. A. 'David's treatment of the Ammonites (2 Samuel 12:31) – A study in the history of interpretation', *TGUOS* 26 (1975–6, but published 1979), 96–107

Schiffmann, I. 'Studien zur Interpretation der neuen phönizischen Inschrift aus Byblos (Byblos 13)', *RSF* 4 (1976), 171–7

Schlögl, N. 'Das Wort *molek* in Inschriften und Bibel', *Wiener Zeitschrift für die Kunde des Morgenlandes* 45 (1938), 203–11

Schmidt, H. *Die grossen Propheten*, 2nd edn (Göttingen, 1924)

Schmökel, H. (ed.) *Kulturgeschichte des alten Orient* (Stuttgart, 1961)

Scholz, P. *Götzendienst und Zauberwesen* (Regensburg, 1877)

Schoors, A. *Jesaja* (Roermond, 1972)

Schroeder, O. *Keilschrifttexte aus Assur verschiedenen Inhalts* (Leipzig, 1920)

Schwab, J. G. 'De Moloch et Remphan' in B. Ugolini (ed.), *Thesaurus Antiquitatum Sacrarum*, vol. 23 (Venice, 1760), pp. 631–44

Scott, R. B. Y. 'The book of Isaiah: chapters 1–39. Introduction and exegesis' in *The Interpreter's Bible*, vol. 5 (New York and Nashville, 1956), pp. 149–381

Selden, J. *De diis Syris* (London, 1617)

Sellin, E. 'Das israelitische Ephod' in C. Bezold (ed.), *Orientalische Studien Theodor Nöldeke zum siebzigsten Geburtstag*, vol. 2 (Giessen, 1906), pp. 699–717

Das Zwölfprophetenbuch, 2nd and 3rd edn (Leipzig, 1929–30)

'Ephod und Terafim', *JPOS* 14 (1934), 185–94

'Noch einmal der alttestamentliche Efod', *JPOS* 17 (1937), 236–51

'Zu Efod und Terafim', *ZAW* 55 (1937), 296–8

Seyrig, H. 'Antiquités syriennes. Héraclès-Nergal', *Syria* 24 (1944–5), 62–80

Simonis, J. *Onomasticum Veteris Testamenti* (Halle, 1741)

Simons, J. *Jerusalem in the Old Testament* (Leiden, 1952)

Skinner, J. *A Critical and Exegetical Commentary on Genesis* (Edinburgh, 1910)

Isaiah I–XXXIX (Cambridge, 1915)

Smith, J. Payne (ed.) *A Compendious Syriac Dictionary* (Oxford, 1903)

Smith, Morton 'A note on burning babies', *JAOS* 95 (1975), 477–9

Smith, R. Payne (ed.) *Thesaurus Syriacus* (2 vols., Oxford, 1879–1901)

Smith, W. R. *Lectures on the Religion of the Semites*, 2nd edn (London, 1894)

The Prophets of Israel, 2nd edn (London, 1919)

Snaith, N. H. 'The Cult of Molech', *VT* 16 (1966), 123–4

Leviticus and Numbers (London, 1967)

Soden, W. von Review of O. Eissfeldt, *Molk als Opferbegriff, ThLZ* 61 (1936), cols. 45f.

Soggin, J. A. '"La tua condotta nella valle", nota a Geremia 2, 23a', *RSO* 36 (1961), 207–11. ET, '"Your conduct in the valley". A Note on Jeremiah 2, 23a', *Old Testament and Oriental Studies* (Rome, 1975), pp. 78–83

'A proposito di sacrifici di fanciulli e di culto dei morti nell' Antico Testamento', *Oriens Antiquus* 8 (1969), 215–17. ET, 'Child sacrifice and the cult of the dead in the Old Testament', *Old Testament and Oriental Studies* (Rome, 1975), pp. 84–7

Judges (ET, London, 1981), 209–13

Spalinger, A. 'A Canaanite ritual found in Egyptian reliefs', *Journal of the Society for the Study of Egyptian Antiquities* 8 (1978), 47–60

Spencer, J. *De Legibus Hebraeorum Ritualibus* (Cambridge, 1685)

Stager, L. E. 'The rite of child sacrifice at Carthage' in J. G. Pedley (ed.), *New Light on Ancient Carthage* (Ann Arbor, 1980), pp. 1–11

'Carthage: a view from the Tophet' in H. G. Niemeyer (ed.), *Phönizier im Westen* (Madrider Beiträge 8, Mainz, 1982), pp. 155–66

Stager, L. E. and Wolff, S. R. 'Child sacrifice at Carthage – religious rite or population control?', *BARev* 10, no. 1 (Jan./Feb., 1984), 31–51

Starcky, J. 'Autour d'une dédicace palmyrénienne à Šadrafa et à Duʿanat. 3. Le sens du mot ḤMN'', *Syria* 26 (1949), 51–5

Stolz, F. *Strukturen und Figuren im Kult von Jerusalem* (*BZAW* 118, 1970)

Tallqvist, K. *Akkadische Götterepitheta* (Helsinki, 1938)

Tetzner, L. *Die Mischna Megilla* (Berlin, 1968)

Thenius, O. *Die Bücher Samuels* (Leipzig, 1842)

Die Bücher de Könige, 2nd edn (Leipzig, 1873)

Thiel, W., *Die deuteronomistische Redaktion von Jeremia 1–25* (*WMANT* 41, Neukirchen-Vluyn, 1973)

Thiersch, H. *Ependytes und Ephod. Gottesbild und Priesterkleid im alten Vorderasien* (Stuttgart, 1936)

Thomas, D. W. 'A consideration of some unusual ways of expressing the superlative in Hebrew', *VT* 3 (1953), 209–24

Tidwell, N. L. 'The linen ephod: 1 Sam. II 18 and 2 Sam. VI 14', *VT* 24 (1974), 505–7

Tiele, C. P. *Vergelijkende Geschiedenis* (Amsterdam, 1872)

Geschiedenis van den Godsdienst in de Oudheid (2 vols., Amsterdam, 1893–1902)

Tomback, R. S. *A Comparative Semitic Lexicon of the Phoenician and Punic Languages* (*SBL* dissertation series 32, Missoula, 1978)

Torrey, C. C. 'On the text of Amos v.26; vi. 1, 2; vii. 2', *JBL* 13 (1894), 61–3

Tov, E. 'L'incidence de la critique textuelle sur la critique littéraire dans le livre de Jérémie', *RB* 79 (1972), 189–99

Tromp, N. J. *Primitive Conceptions of Death and the Nether World in the Old Testament* (Rome, 1969)

Tronchetti, C. 'Per la cronologia del tophet di S. Antico', *RSF* 7 (1979), 201–5

Tsevat, M. 'Ishbosheth and congeners: the names and their study', *HUCA* 46 (1975), 71–87

Tur-Sinai, N. H. (=Torczyner, H.) הלשון והספר (3 vols., Jerusalem, 1948)
Vahlen, J. *Ennianae poesis reliquiae*, 2nd edn (Leipzig, 1903)
Vaux, R. de Review of O. Eissfeldt, *Molk als Opferbegriff*, *RB* 45 (1936), 278–82
'Les Prophètes de Baal sur le Mont Carmel', *Bulletin du Musée de Beyrouth* 5 (1941), 7–20; reprinted in *Bible et Orient* (Paris, 1967), pp. 485–97. ET, *The Bible and the Ancient Near East* (Garden City, 1971), pp. 238–51
Les Institutions de l'Ancien Testament (2 vols., Paris, 1958–60). ET, *Ancient Israel*, 2nd edn (London, 1965)
Les Sacrifices de l'Ancien Testament (Paris, 1964). ET, *Studies in Old Testament Sacrifice* (Cardiff, 1964)
Vermes, G. 'Leviticus 18:21 in ancient Jewish Bible exegesis' in J. J. Petuchowski and E. Fleischer (eds.), *Studies in Aggadah, Targum and Jewish Liturgy in Memory of Joseph Heinemann* (Jerusalem, 1981), pp. 108–24
Wade, G. W. *The Book of the Prophet Isaiah* (London, 1911)
Weinfeld, M. 'The worship of Molech and of the Queen of Heaven and its background', *UF* 4 (1972), 133–54
'Burning babies in ancient Israel. A rejoinder to Morton Smith's article in *JAOS* 95 (1975), pp. 477–479', *UF* 10 (1978), 411–13
Wenham, G. J. *The Book of Leviticus* (London, 1979)
Wernberg-Møller, P. 'Two notes', *VT* 8 (1958), 305–8
Westermann, C. *Das Buch Jesaia Kapitel 40–66* (Göttingen, 1966). ET, *Isaiah 40–66* (London, 1969)
Wevers, J. W. *Ezekiel* (London, 1969)
Whitaker, J. I. S. *Motya* (London, 1921)
Whybray, R. N. *Isaiah 40–66* (London, 1975)
Wildberger, H. *Jesaja* (3 vols., Neukirchen-Vluyn, 1972–82; vol. 1, 2nd edn, 1980)
Wiseman, D. J. *The Alalakh Tablets* (London, 1953)
Wiseman, D. J. and Wilson, J. V. Kinnier 'The Nimrud tablets, 1950', *Iraq* 13 (1951), 102–22
Wits (Witsius), H. *Miscellaneorum sacrorum libri iv*, 2nd edn (2 vols., Amsterdam, 1695–1700)
Wolff, H. W. *Dodekapropheton 1 Hosea*, 2nd edn (Neukirchen-Vluyn, 1965). ET, *Hosea* (Philadelphia, 1974)
Dodekapropheton 2 Joel und Amos, 2nd edn (Neukirchen-Vluyn, 1975). ET, *Joel and Amos* (Philadelphia, 1977)
Wood, W. C. 'The religion of Canaan (concluded)', *JBL* 35 (1916), 163–279
Wright, G. H. B. *The Book of Job* (London and Edinburgh, 1883)
Xella, P. 'Un testo ugaritico recente (*RS* 24.266, *Verso*, 9–19) e il "sacrificio dei primi nati"', *RSF* 6 (1978), 127–36

Ziegra, C. S. 'De crudelissima liberorum immolatione Molocho facta' in B. Ugolini, *Thesaurus Antiquitatum Sacrarum*, vol. 23 (Venice, 1760), pp. 887–924

Zimmerli, W. *Ezechiel* (2 vols., Neukirchen-Vluyn, 1969). ET, *Ezekiel* (2 vols., Philadelphia, 1979–83)

Zimmern, H. *Beiträge zur Kenntnis der babylonischen Religion* (Leipzig, 1896)

INDEX OF OLD TESTAMENT REFERENCES

INDEX OF AUTHORS